What Children Remember

A MEMOIR BY TASHA SHANEL HUNTER

FIRST EDITION

Printed in the United States of America
www.tashahunterauthor.com

Paperback: ISBN 978-1-7344178-9-0
Hardcover ISBN: 978-1-7344178-7-6
eBook ISBN: 978-1-7344178-8-3

Tasha Hunter books may be purchased for educational, business, or sales promotional use. For information, please email the author at tashahunterauthor@gmail.com.

Library of Congress Control Number: 2020902379

TABLE OF CONTENTS

I dedicate this book to Myrtle Ester Hill. I've always known I would spend the rest of my life honoring you. Thank you for loving me.

Disclaimer

This is a work of creative nonfiction. The events are portrayed to the best of my recollection. While all the stories in this book represent my truth, names and other identifying details about those individuals who were a part of my journey have been changed. In most cases, I have compressed events and changed the names of exact locations in order to protect the privacy of those involved. I did not write my story to cause shame or embarrassment to family members who are still a part of my story today. I wrote my book, and I tell my story in order to free myself from years of shame-based secrecy and to cast a light on the darkness of child abuse.

INTRO

"The lion's story will never be known as long as the hunter is the one who tells it."

~UNKNOWN

This book is my story and my recollection of childhood and young adult experiences which shaped the self-possessed and fully awoken woman I am today. With honesty, transparency, and vulnerability, I have dared to speak about my past. Telling my truth has meant reliving some of my most horrifyingly painful memories. Through my writing process, I found a constructive way to overcome my fear and apprehension about personal disclosures by envisioning those women who may see themselves reflected in my story—women who are still living in shame and suffering in silence. I wanted to write a book that transcends age, race, religion, and socioeconomic status because child abuse is found in every corner of the world. In writing this book, my goals remained clear to inspire and to encourage women from all walks of life. There is strength to be had and resolve to be experienced beyond the pain of insufferable shame and silence. It is possible, because I am possible. This book has been written for women who think the horror of their experiences is beyond the reach of God's grace. I hope my story will resonate, inspire, uplift, and give readers HOPE. I testify as a witness for myself and for others that it is possible to overcome seemingly insurmountable circumstances and to forge and possess a future which represents the best of who you are. The past does not dictate your future. You may not yet believe the truth of this powerful statement, so it bears repeating: *the past does not dictate your future.* What you *choose* to do with the experiences that have plagued and scarred you, will help give birth to the success of your future.

The hardest part of recounting the experiences of my life has been the arduous process of inching my way forward on this emotional tightrope of speaking my truth, while protecting the ones who (central to my recovery) have robustly inspired me—and challenged me—to share the details of my life with candid honesty. In the process of writing my book, I have felt high-strung, heart-palpitating emotions arising from the fear of judgment by people who knew me at certain points of my life, and by extension, think they know who I am now.

What kept me writing in spite of the fear of scrutiny is remembering the little girl I was who desperately needed to hear this exact story—for every girl who feels utterly alone on an emotional island, emotionally battered and spent while waiting for a noble cavalry to rescue her and fight on her behalf. Even now, as a fully actualized adult who knows the value of my contributions, while writing the book, I still imagined the text and phone conversations this book might elicit among my family and friends: "Girl, did you know she did that? Why would she share that? She should have taken that one to the grave." These doubts held me captive until I stamped them out by taking full authorship of my story. This memoir isn't written for the critics—it's for those of you who are reading this book because you recognize that a part of your personal story is also a part of mine. This is a book for those of us who are tired of hiding. On my very best days, of which I am now blessed to have many, I never neglect to recognize that I am still that little girl who appears on the following pages. She is all of me, not separate from me, and this is *our* truth.

HEAVENLY FATHER

Thank you for making it possible for me to tell my story today. I pray it is representative of the message you have called me to share. Those times in my life when I felt like a failure, you called me a success. When I labeled myself as a victim, you taught me how to survive. Thank you for using my life to empower, heal, uplift, and educate others. I am grateful for each and every person you've sent into my life to help me on my journey. I pray you bless each person reading my story. Bless those of my sisters who feel lost, left out, forgotten, and unloved.

In Jesus' name, I pray.
Amen.

CHAPTER I

The 11ᵗʰ Year

"When my father and my mother forsake me, then the Lord will take me up."

~PSALM 27:10 (KJV)

"Be ready to get a beating when I get home." This is what my mother, Katrina, said to me in a phone call that would change the trajectory of my life forever. While the beatings I endured were commonplace, this turning point was an act of defiance in which I learned the importance of standing up for myself. At the time, I was just a few months shy of my eighteenth birthday and tired of well-meaning adults asking me boring questions such as, *So, what are you gonna do after high school?* I had no idea, seeing as how every fiber in my body was exhausted to the brink of collapse from the daily struggle of just trying to get by. I didn't have time to lay out a well-developed plan for the next four years of what people called *adulthood*.

During my senior year at North Pulaski High School, I was failing chemistry. I had tried unsuccessfully to study atoms, positive and negative ions, and kinetic theory. But when studying failed, I placed a cheat sheet inside of my TI-85 calculator. On the day of my exam, my teacher, a petite brunette named Ms. Ricci, was surveying the room and picked up on the awkward way I was covering my calculator. Leaning forward, she discovered the cheat sheet between my forearm and chest. She snatched my test from me and instructed me to wait after class. With a disapproving look, she said, "Latasha, I cannot believe you cheated on my test. You are getting an F. You'll have to go to summer school if you want to graduate."

Grabbing my backpack, I left the room in a spell of panic, my mind hard at work devising a plan. During the last week of school, I told the secretary I would be moving from my middle-class neighborhood in Gravel Ridge, Arkansas to some other address. I made one up on the fly, hoping I would be gone, long gone, by the time the postal employee marked the school's letter with *return to sender*. Thinking back, I didn't lie—in fact, I predicted my future.

My mother, who seemed to care more about my grades than me, became suspicious about not receiving my final report card, so she contacted the school. I imagined they were confused and apologetic regarding the mistake. My mother was quite good at putting two and two together when she wanted to, and her finding out about my grades didn't surprise me. Almost eighteen, I relished the idea that my days living at home with her were numbered, but I wasn't yet ready to move out— I had no plan B, and I hadn't planned for her to find out about my failing grade so early.

During the eleven years when I lived with my mother, I feared her more than I feared God. She had an incredibly harsh tongue and expletives like "that mothafucka" or "son of a bitch" sprang forth from her mouth on a regular basis. Intuitively, I knew my life and my being her daughter meant little to nothing to her. For years, whenever she lashed out in anger, she would tell me, "I never wanted you. Bitch. Whore." She never once kissed me, or hugged me, or affirmed our relationship as mother and daughter in any way. My body existed in a state of chronic angst. I was so jittery and jumpy all the time that I developed nervous habits like biting my nails until they bled. As I waited for her to come home on the day she discovered I had deceived her with respect to my report card, I sat quietly in my bedroom in a mauve, formal, dining chair mulling over my options. For years, I'd wondered why she had put this out-of-place dining chair in my bedroom. The chair belonged somewhere else, kind of like me.

I heard a car door slam; she was home. Her keys jangled as she unlocked the front door. I could feel her presence as she walked down the hall, first stopping into her bedroom to say *hello* to her husband, Darryl. Afterwards, she carefully shut the door. Every time she beat me, she made sure to spare Darryl of any involvement by closing their door before heading to mine. I always figured her shutting their door gave him an excuse to remain silent about the abuse going on under our roof.

She entered my room, and I sat rigidly with my back pressed against the misplaced dining room chair, looking at her sour complexion as she droned on and on, first battering me with her abusive words. I sat anxious, all the more fearful of what I knew was coming, as it always inevitably did. I readied my face to be slapped, and a part of me disassociated, as a way to protect myself. I no longer heard her toxic words—I only saw her lips moving, as she continued to yell at me. Antagonizing me, she got in my face, bending down to be eye level with me, and pointed her long, shimmery, pink, acrylic nail at my nose. If I could have melted into the chair at that moment, I would have. She continued yelling obscenities nonstop for a few dreadful minutes. Then, she finally left the room to retrieve her whipping belt, the same one she had used on me multiple times before. The thick, embossed, leather belt was her weapon of choice. She found macabre pleasure in telling me that she'd had this belt made by inmates at the local penitentiary. In the past, I would scream in agony whenever she used it, squirming on the edge of the bed, my exposed body twisting in reaction to the sharp pain, and flopping helplessly to avoid impact. Each strike that my mother landed always seemed to embolden her. She took a stance of superiority, and the power she lorded over me seemed to feed her arrogance. These beatings were the only time my mother ever touched me when I was growing up. She beat me while quoting scripture, saying, "I'm doing this for your own good." She even went so far as to call the beatings "love," and cited Proverbs 13:24. The welts on my skin, fresh after each beating, were the only physical emblem of the love she claimed to have for me. As I grew older, I dealt with pain every time I made a point of re-examining my broken life, in the light of my broken upbringing.

I knew I had to take a stand. It was tonight, or never at all. Nearly an adult, I no longer wished to endure the role of the submissive, terrified, little girl who lived in day-to-day fear of these beatings. I shakily got up from the chair and made my way to the dresser mirror where I rehearsed what I would say to her. I intended to look her in the eyes as I spoke. She commanded me to undress and lay across my bed as she had done many times before.

Taking a deep breath, I refused to budge an inch from where I stood, and staring back at her, I somehow found the courage to say, "You have no right to beat me. You yourself lie, cheat, and steal. You do the very same things you punish me for doing." I searched her face for a reaction. Something in her dislodged, and she was visibly taken aback by my assertion.

She lowered her voice to a whisper, and through gritted teeth she hissed, "You betta lower your voice before Darryl wakes up." Hmmm, I thought, not the response I expected. We both knew he wasn't asleep and, in that moment, I saw a crack in her veneer for the first time. Katrina had cheated on Darryl more times than I can count. Despite her frequent infidelities, she still veiled the truth from him and didn't want Darryl to find out. After so many years of feeling helpless at the hands of Katrina, for this rare moment, I had leverage over her. I knew she would do anything to keep me from outing her to Darryl about her sexual indiscretions. After a few more tense moments, which I thought would never end, she acquiesced. With a sense of finality, she said, "If I can't whoop you, you can't live in my house."

I didn't know what to do; my mind went momentarily blank, and then I felt frantic all of a sudden. Aunt Dorris, who was the closest Katrina ever had to a mother figure, was a presence in my mother's life when her own biological mother couldn't be. At that point in my young life, I had few role models I could turn to in trust, and Aunt Dorris was the only person I knew to call at that moment. When she answered the phone, I told her what happened and that I needed a place to stay until I could sort myself out.

Aunt Dorris was in her early sixties with a head of silver, shoulder-length hair and a wide, full figure. As black families go, she might have been called "Big Momma" or "Madear," but I just called her *Aunt Dorris*. She had been a much-needed, positive influence in my mother's life; Katrina was only four when her own mother, who was Aunt Dorris's sister, suddenly died. Life dealt my mother another emotional blow when, at the age of sixteen, her father also passed away from health complications. While Aunt Dorris was well-meaning, Katrina's problems were often larger than the both of them, and she could not provide the stability that was woefully lacking in Katrina's adolescent years.

A devout Christian, Aunt Dorris was a conservative woman who carried a Bible with her everywhere she went. She depended on her faith in God and trusted in his promise of salvation. After I was born, Aunt Dorris remained a distant relative whom I didn't have contact with and whom I didn't know during my earliest years with my father's family in Pine Bluff, Arkansas. I never lacked for love and affection from my paternal grandmother who raised me when I was an infant, but after the age of six, when Katrina regained custody and came back into my life, I often desperately longed for the warmth and intimacy which my own mother could not provide. Aunt Dorris liked to rationalize my mother's callous, cold, behavior by saying, on more than one occasion, "You know I've known your mom since the day my sister delivered her. She probably wouldn't be this way if she'd had her mother."

Over time, Aunt Dorris became more candid with me and shared more and more of the painful details surrounding my mother's upbringing. Each event and each new source of trauma seemed to have negatively impacted Katrina's ability to fully become a well-adjusted, actualized person. When I thought of it this way, I couldn't help but feel empathy for her. What if she'd had two healthy, supportive, and loving parents? How might have her life, and by extension my own, been different? When Katrina became pregnant with me, Aunt Dorris strongly urged my mother to keep me. As a member of the Pentecostal Holiness Church, Aunt Dorris was austere in her faith, and she believed in specific roles for women. She dressed modestly in loose-fitting, ankle-length dresses and suits. She was the living embodiment of Peter 3:3 which says, "Do not let your adorning be external—the braiding of hair and the putting on of gold jewelry, or the clothing you wear—but let your adorning be the hidden person of the heart with the imperishable beauty of a gentle and quiet spirit, which in God's sight is very precious." In Arkansas, we called women like her *sanctified*.

There were times when I was growing up that Aunt Dorris tried to counsel my mother, which Katrina felt particularly at odds with. Whenever Aunt Dorris gave me advice, the conversations we had usually centered around my role as a child and the importance of letting things go, forgiving, and honoring one's mother and father. On more than one occasion, she recited Exodus 20:12 to me, a verse used to remind children to respect their parents. Aunt Dorris's guidance, based mostly on biblical inter-pretation and long-held traditions within the black com-munity, fell short of the mark and left me feeling as if she didn't care or truly understand how I felt. At no time did she give me permission to simply feel hurt or acknowledge how the devastation in my upbringing had impacted me.

Parted from my father's close-knit family, by the age of eighteen, I had only Aunt Dorris to call on as my next of kin. She came to my rescue, even though calling Aunt Dorris left me with a sickening feeling in my gut, as I speculated about the future. As the only other living soul I knew to turn to for help, I told Aunt Dorris to please hurry, "She's kicking me out." After expressing some initial hesitation, Aunt Dorris agreed to come get me. In that moment, I was left to wonder if I was betraying any loyalty Aunt Dorris had towards my mother. In all the years I'd lived with Katrina after she was granted primary custody, I never asked Aunt Dorris for a single thing but this time I was in desperate need of her aid. As I hastily gathered my belongings, my mother, half in disbelief, followed me around the house as I packed.

When Katrina saw me grab a large black suitcase from the bottom of my closet, she yanked it from my hands, trying to reassert her power by humiliating me in the moments leading up to my exodus, saying, "You aren't taking anything out of this house that I bought." She snatched the luggage from me and emptied my belongings into a trash bag.

When Aunt Dorris arrived, she found me anxiously waiting for her in the backyard patio of the house which I'd no longer call my home. Seeing me so vulnerable in that moment, she said with resignation, "I told her a long time ago that she'd better stop mistreating you. I tried to warn her that once she lost you, it would be forever." And then a long, quiet pause hung in the air between us, after which she added, "You're not coming back, are you?"

Too choked up to say a word, I just shook my head *no*. I knew nothing about my future except that I would never return to the broken life Katrina had given me. Aunt Dorris continued to explain, "She made more of an effort with your older brother. She tried to do her best with Anthony, but she couldn't give him a good home life either. It's not your fault that she ended up mistreating you."

When we left shortly thereafter, Katrina did not emerge to say *goodbye*, or even to watch us leave. Having nothing more to say to her, I felt apprehension about what would become of me, but I had no regret in leaving her behind. Aunt Dorris shut the door behind us, as I passed the threshold into the next chapter of my future.

Within a couple of days of moving into Aunt Dorris's home, I befriended my aunt's daughter, Reva, who was raising two young children but still lived at home. I could never understand why an adult-child would volitionally choose to live with a parent. Maybe because I was so mistreated in my own childhood, I often asked myself, *Why on earth would anyone choose to stay at home—when a prize of adulthood is living in your own place and having the freedom to go wherever you'd like?*

Meanwhile, Katrina took no time at all to send Aunt Dorris the rest of my belongings— mostly clothes I didn't want or that didn't fit me anymore. I gave away what few material possessions I had. Given that Aunt Dorris was

actually my mother's aunt and my great-aunt, Reva and
Katrina were the same age growing up and had a tumultuous relationship, similar to rival siblings. Reva retold
one pronounced memory of having an argument with my
mother which resulted in one of them pulling a knife on
the other. Reva was thirty-seven the year I moved in with
her and Aunt Dorris for what turned out to be a brief,
month-long stay, while I figured out my next step; maybe
I would call my estranged father, Maurice, in Colorado.
He'd settled down with his long-time girlfriend, with
whom he'd had another daughter.

In the immediate days following the exodus from
my mom's house, Katrina, who was in denial about my
emancipation, showed up at Aunt Dorris's place to terror-
ize me. It would be a long time before I was completely
free from her clutches. She would bang on Aunt Dorris's
closed windows and locked doors. She was stark raving
mad, stalking me. Reva's young children were alarmed by
seeing such behavior, and watched curiously between the
window blinds, as she marched around the perimeter of
the house shouting, "Come to the damn door, bitch. I'm
gonna beat your ass. You think you can run from me?"

Like a scene out of the movie *Friday the 13th*, and
seeing that Katrina could not be placated, the kids and I
ducked out of sight by huddling together on Aunt Dorris's
linoleum floor in an area between the bathroom and
the bedroom. Even though I was safe inside the house,
Katrina could petrify me, and my body started to tremble
in reaction to her threats. In a state of high alarm, I could

hear the sound of my heart pounding, and I wished to myself again and again, *please, forget about me.* This marked the first, but not the only occasion, she appeared to brutally harass me. She kept up this reappearing act for quite a while, and it drove me to wonder if her motivations were purely selfish. After all, if people asked about me, how would she explain my whereabouts? More than the fear of losing me, I felt she feared losing face.

Reva was a comfort to me during my temporary stay at Aunt Dorris's. There was plenty to vent about, and when Reva rehashed old memories she had of my mother, it helped me to keep things in perspective. I felt a small bond with Reva due to our mutual disdain for Katrina. Reva stepped in to help me with the occasional favor. I tried to thank her in any way I knew how. I had a little bit of money saved up from my jobs at CiCi's Pizza and Harvest Foods. About $3,000 accumulated in a savings account that I had left untouched. A small portion of the money paid for gas and my portion of the utilities. After all, I wasn't accustomed to people pausing their lives to care for me. It had been years since anyone had.

CHAPTER 2

#13

"There are poisons that blind you, and poisons that open your eyes."

~AUGUST STRINDBERG

I've often thought if I could only understand Katrina better, I would be one step closer to understanding the puzzle of my own identity. *Are the character traits I detest in her, whether biological or environmental, also an immutable part of me? Am I doomed to repeat history by making the same mistakes as my mother based purely on our biological connection?* Now as an adult, when I listen to the cadence and sound of my adult voice, I'm often keenly aware of how I come across strong and forceful – much like Katrina's voice – which reverberated through the walls at home whenever she would raise her voice. Despite the similarities which show that I am my mother's daughter, I often stop to remind myself (with a much-needed gut check) that she and I are otherwise nothing alike.

As time passed, the more remote distance I could put between Katrina and me, the better I was able to develop a sense of compassion for how unprepared she was to raise me. Her life became increasingly unstable after the death of both of her parents prior to her sixteenth birthday. By the age of fourteen, she'd given birth to my brother, Anthony, and I made my arrival four years later. With two kids to raise, though she was just a kid herself, she didn't get the chance to graduate from high school, but she did obtain her GED.

She never had any sense of security as she bounced from home to home. I later learned she suffered the additional trauma of sexual assault on more than one occasion, a reprehensible violation of the physical body which would scar my life as well. She witnessed first-hand the devastating effects of substance abuse, mental illness, and incest which were rife within our lineage. She lived in chaos with no point of reference for what safety looked or felt like. Katrina experienced loss in life at a rate that did not give her time to heal.

Aunt Dorris and Reva described my mom's adolescence as being wild and out of control; no one could tell her what to do. A strong-willed child, she wouldn't listen to anyone and disregarded anything and everything coming from her elders. While rebellion is sometimes of youth, believing we know it all and don't need to seek or receive help from anyone, my mom never outgrew the shortcomings of her youthful temperament. Her personality in adulthood was characterized by impulsivity, poor judgement, aggression, and a total disregard for the feelings of those she disparaged. Maybe she lived life at such a frenetic pace that she didn't have the frame of mind to stop, internalize, and reflect on the abusive legacy of her decisions. The life she created for herself didn't afford her much opportunity to love well and be wholly loved in return. Painful life experiences and the associated hurt she endured, became the prism through which she saw her life. Having experienced more than her share of pain she, in turn, hurt and inflicted pain on others. Maybe the hurt was all she'd ever known about love.

I often wondered what my birth truly represented to my mother. Did my face remind her of someone she'd rather forget? Did my existence remind her of a trauma she'd wished she'd escaped but didn't? If I'd come to be as a result of a violent act such as rape, I could then justify my mother's vitriol. Or if she'd been pressured to carry me to term out of condemnation from Aunt Dorris and other family members, I could better understand why she felt no maternal bond towards me. Katrina never candidly shared the events surrounding my conception. She told me once that she'd been pregnant five times and birthed three: my older brother Anthony, me, and a baby who failed to thrive and then died in the hospital's NICU before ever having a chance to come home. I imagine she

worried constantly about a multitude of things with education, money problems, instability, and lack of support
being at the top of her list. I imagine she felt alone and
hopeless much of the time, with none of the coping skills
necessary to help her navigate successfully through the
competitive world at large.

Without the necessary resources to care for me, a few
months after my birth, she paid a visit to Ms. Earnestine
and Mr. John Hines, the parents of my estranged father,
Maurice. My parents had a passionate but short-lived
fling, and their stormy relationship didn't last. After my
birth, they mutually agreed to give custodial responsibilities to Maurice's mother when it became painfully
obvious they were in no position to care for me.

My grandparents lived in Pine Bluff, Arkansas, a small
town which became the formative setting of most of the
memories I carry of early childhood. My paternal grandmother, Ernestine, was the caretaker who I exclusively
called "Momma" from a young age. At times throughout
the earlier years of my troubled adult life, I would cling
to a sense of nostalgia I still had for Arkansas and my
earliest familial experiences while growing up there.

Speaking of the evening when I arrived as a swaddled
infant, the story my Momma relays to me is indescrib-
ably awful. Katrina walked through the doorway and
promptly took a seat in the living room, as if she were
getting ready to confront Maurice's mother in some way.
Momma looked around confused and asked her, "Where
is the baby?" Apparently, my mother stonewalled the

question directed at her and didn't respond. "Girl, what's wrong with you?" Momma recalled raising her voice and asking once more.

"She's outside," was all Katrina finally said.

Momma responded, "*Outside*?! She's not a dog! Go get her!"

Becoming a war of wills, when Katrina didn't show any signs of rising from her seat, Momma again begged her to go and fetch me from the frigid, night air. She remembered it being cold enough that evening to have the heat on inside the house. With Momma's common sense intact, she took the initiative to yank open her front door, and there, she found me garmented in nothing other than a swaddling blanket and diapers. As Momma bent down to pick me up, Katrina charged past her and left without a word of goodbye. In that moment of exchange, when it was uncertain as to whether Katrina would ever have the necessary means to reclaim me as her own daughter, some part of her sense of self was surrendered and indelibly lost that evening.

Before hearing Momma's account of past events, I'd always created a homecoming fantasy in my juvenile mind that somehow an oversized stork delivered me in a woven bassinet with a hand-written note from the heavens. The cold, harsh reckoning of actual events pains me, and when I envision the neglectful way I was left outside her door, a tide of sadness washes over me to this day.

Now in her eighties, Momma forgets what she ate for supper yesterday, but when asked about the events of my childhood, she is able to recall them vividly. "What did it feel like to have a baby in the house again, after having raised your own children?" I asked. When I tentatively asked this question, I was really asking if she harbored any anger about my being there, and whether she ever felt burdened by my presence. Momma reassured me calling me a "good, good, girl." She added, "You were smart and aware of everything. Everybody loved you."

She howled, as she recalled a time when she walked through the grocery store parking lot and a woman asked, "Ms. Hines, you done gone and had another one? Is that your baby?"

She replied, "Yes, she is my child." Even though she hadn't given birth to me, she loved me like I was one of her own. She nicknamed me *Nikki* when I was a baby. Other times, she called me *Tash*, a name my close friends still use. Loving me as her own even in to my adulthood, she would speak about my upbringing, filling me with gratitude for her maternal instincts. I never detected any hint of resentment or feel that she battled with the responsibilities of caring for me – although she may have.

When I was a child, I remember Momma as a towering 5'2" with a stout frame and legs as skinny and fragile as twigs. I looked up to her. No matter the day, she wore a muumuu, a housecoat, or an apron around her waist until it was time for bed. Her life was filled with the same rituals day in and day out. One quaint childhood memory I have is walking into the bathroom and seeing Momma standing in front of her sink brushing her teeth

with baking soda and gargling with the gold-colored
Listerine—the kind that burned. Rather than smelling
like White Diamonds perfume or the fresh scent of clean
linen, she had a musty odor that is common in the elderly.
On Sundays, even after bathing and dousing herself in
Avon products, she still carried the unsparing scent of
struggle. As far as I could tell, she had never known what
it was to pamper herself with pedicures or massages. She
spent the great majority of each day toiling with an endless
list of domestic chores. Washing the dishes, tending to her
garden, and preparing our daily meals commandeered all
of her time. She worked all day, every day, all the days of
her adult life—there was no Sabbath for the homemakers,
housewives, and stay-at-home moms.

She was the only authentic, strong, maternal figure I
knew, but I was by no means the sole recipient of her parenting skills. In addition to having several of her twelve
children return to the nest and live with her as adults, she
supported a half dozen grandchildren with the level of
engagement one might expect from a parent, not a grand-
parent. She found her self-worth in serving her family,
taking care of them and loving them the best way she
knew how. Once I was old enough to have conversations
with Momma, I noted her idiosyncrasies and the way she
carried herself in a conversation. No matter the topic
at hand, she often responded by saying, "My goodness
gracious." And when someone would say something she
didn't quite know how to respond to, she would simply
reply, "I shul say."

In the six years I lived with Momma, I also got to know Grandpa, and a few of my father's siblings including my Aunt Yolanda, Aunt Gloria, Aunt Faye, and Uncle Donny. My dad and Uncle Donny took after grandpa, as the strong and silent type. While grandpa was a part of our household, he mostly kept to himself. While it felt natural for me to call my paternal grandmother *Momma*, I never called Grandpa *Dad* because I didn't see him that way. I used to fear him until he opened his mouth and laughed, revealing his thick, fleshy, pink gums. Although I knew he loved me, he didn't nurture me in the same way as Momma. I can't recall a single conversation I had with him. But I enjoyed his company.

One vivid memory I *do* have of my grandpa is seeing him stretched out, all 6'2" of him, in his favorite recliner. He often wore oversized denim overalls and the kind of clothes that made him look like a farmin', hard-workin', from-the-country man. He always carried a small black comb in his pocket, as if it were a part of his uniform. Nightly, he would hold his comb up in the air, and he'd say, "Who wants to comb my hair today?" My cousins and I took turns completing the task, as he allowed himself to be groomed while seated in his comfy recliner.

Asking Momma to recount those early years she said, "Your granddaddy always made sure we all had enough to eat." Between the garden and the government rations of milk, cheese, peanut butter, and canned ham we had *plenty*. We grew collard greens, butter beans, squash, and purple hull peas in the garden—you name it, and we grew it. During the summers in Pine Bluff, my cousins and I picked pecans, shucked corn, and ate the juiciest, most delicious watermelons. Momma canned vegetables and ground pork for hog's head cheese. I awoke each morning to the aroma of sausage, bacon, eggs, and biscuits. We never lacked for anything to eat, and there was always something good cooking in the house. My favorite dessert was Momma's homemade rice pudding, which she often served with hot cocoa in warm milk in the evenings to help me fall asleep.

My earliest memory of my dad, Maurice, was when I was four-years old. I sat on the couch waiting on Momma to finish cooking breakfast. Maurice sat opposite me, the wonderful aroma of mom's hearty vittles filling our nostrils. Maurice hollered into the kitchen, "Fix me up some rice, too, Mom. Don't forget the butter." I remember being seated with my legs crossed under me on the couch that day, just watching my dad intently. I was hoping he would say something to me. But he didn't. While I didn't feel wrongfully ignored by my father at that age, I didn't feel seen either. Engaging me and getting to know me was obviously not of any paternal interest to him, and this communication gap which existed since my earliest memory of him would only widen as time passed.

Of my Dad's brothers, the uncle I looked up to the most was Uncle Donny. Unlike his sister, Yolanda, who chose to live with Momma most of her adult life, as soon as Uncle Donny was of age, he left Arkansas to serve in the Air Force. He eventually got married and raised two sons. When he visited, something about his straightened military posture and the way he always acknowledged me with a bright smile made me immediately love him. One vivid memory I have of him, and one of my most cherished, is of him teasing me by placing his hand on top of my head in a playful and affectionate way. It was the only time in my life someone had acknowledged me in that way, as a joyful little girl with an infectious smile. That one-second interaction of being truly seen and truly loved for who I was in that moment of time is one of my fondest memories.

I got to know my Aunt Yolanda the best. She is the youngest of Momma's children and was a teenager when I moved in with them in Pine Bluff. I stayed in touch with Aunt Yolanda, and years later, she recalled me as a young child saying, "You enjoyed being around family. You were a quiet and inquisitive child; you observed everything and everyone. Most of your time was spent around adults, so you acted like one."

Well, into my own adulthood, Yolanda was always a great historian helping me to recall events and memories about my life as a child. Perhaps, acquiring the strong example of nurturing that Momma embodied throughout her life, Yolanda, like her mother, selflessly took care of others including her aging parents and her many nieces and nephews.

As a teenager, Yolanda frequently helped Momma take care of me by babysitting, feeding me, and combing my hair. Perhaps, that's why my memories with her are the most well-remembered. She and I shared the same thick coils of black hair. She often wore hers in a short Afro. With her innate comedic ability, Yolanda's the comic relief in the family. She's always able to bring levity to any situation. She's the kind of person who can make you burst into laughter while you're crying. I know of only one other person who is able to do that, and I later fell in love with him.

Soon after his break-up with Katrina, Maurice joined the Army. Momma said, "They stayed together for a while but eventually went their separate ways." None of my family members could provide sufficiently good details about my father's whereabouts between the time I was born and my first, four-year-old memory of him. Momma said, "Maurice used to live here for a while, and one day I looked up and he had told Katrina she could live here, too. I told him he can't just move somebody in *my* house. So, I kicked them both out." They left and found a small apartment. She said, "All I asked is they have some respect. I don't believe in people shacking up."

Beyond that, Momma didn't have a great deal to share regarding his parental involvement in my life. I got the impression from Momma that he checked in from time to time but didn't parent, not even for the part-time responsibilities of feeding, holding, playing, or bathing. According to Aunt Yolanda's recollection, however, there were moments shared with my father in which he was very involved. She said he doted on me, bought me cute dresses, and carried me in his arms like a little burrito.

I was comforted in knowing there were moments he held and adored me, because for long stretches of my youth and adolescence he was entirely absent. There were times while growing up that were so deafeningly devoid of his parental involvement, that I felt like he'd forgotten I even existed.

I vividly recall the last night he was in Pine Bluff before moving to Colorado, where he would eventually settle long-term. I was four, and I awoke to find my father lying next to me, enveloping my small frame in a protective manner. Lifting my head from the pillow, I thought, *When did he get here? My daddy's in bed with me.* Puzzled but comforted by his presence, I turned back around and tried to recapture the happiness of the moment while pretending to be asleep. I wanted him to hold me like this forever. As far as I could remember, he'd never been so near to my heart. But within a few seconds, he rolled over and pushed the comforter off his body in haste, as if he'd overslept. Getting up from a position of cradling me, he jetted to the bathroom. As I listened to the shower running, I wondered if he'd return. I wanted him to talk to me and engage me affectionately. I remember missing him while he was in the bathroom as I wafted in and out of light sleep.

The next thing I knew, I overheard him in the living room talking to Momma. I could hear her asking for clarification on times and when he would be arriving somewhere. There were few words exchanged, and the moment felt absent of any emotion. Confused, I popped out of bed and ran into the living room, worried he might leave me without saying goodbye.

"Where are you going?" I said, noticing a suitcase by the door.

He replied, "I'm moving to Colorado with my girlfriend."

Shocked and heartbroken, something moved me to take my final steps towards him and stand before him in the totality of who I was. I took one last, long, look peering into him and thought, *Why didn't anyone tell me? If I hadn't gotten out of bed, he would have left without saying a word.* Within minutes, his girlfriend had arrived and pulled into the driveway. She didn't come inside, but when he heard her car outside, he looked at Momma and said, "I love you. I'll call you when I arrive in Denver."

Like my mother on the day she dropped me off at Momma's, he didn't give me a last kiss, a goodbye, or any explanation of when I'd see him again. If I'd had the presence of mind and thought quickly, I would have held onto his leg and pleaded for more time together. In that moment, he treated me with the emotional distance and apathy one might have for a next-door neighbor's kid, not your own child. His abrupt exit from my life made me ask myself, *Is that man my daddy or not? 'Cause he don't act like my daddy.*

I don't know if either of my parents thought about the impact their departure would have on me. What led them to determine they were better off without me? As much as I loved Momma and my whole family in Pine Bluff, none of them filled the void caused by knowing my parents had chosen life without me. Was there something I couldn't see and something I didn't know that made me unlovable? Their decisions during that pivotal time in my life set a precedent for how I interpreted my own worth in the future. When a child rejected my friendship or an adult did anything to me that I interpreted as embarrassing, demeaning, or inconsiderate, I questioned whether my life mattered. If my parents don't love me, why would anyone else? When I was an adult and my friends drifted away, I convinced myself it was because I didn't deserve them or wasn't good enough for them. My parents' departures created chronic, lifelong difficulties with trusting others.

Although I felt an appreciation and a fullness for my family life with Momma in Pine Bluff, as time passed, and as I became more aware, I also began experiencing feelings of profound emptiness for the first time. Despite this internal struggle which was beginning to wage a war inside of me, I was otherwise a happy-go-lucky child externally. Whereas, Katrina and Maurice failed to be present for a lot of personal firsts, such as my first day of kindergarten, Momma and my aunts stood-in as my surrogate family, and I thank God they loved me so well.

I remember learning my ABCs sitting at the table on my knees in Momma's living room with a number two pencil in hand and plenty of erasers nearby. I practiced writing sight words, spelling my name, and rehearsing my address. Walking past me with her arms full of laundry, Momma said, "Sit down and learn that by heart. You can't start school if you don't know that stuff." I was mischievous and wore a playful grin as I practiced. The faster I wrote my name and recited my address, the faster I could get back to watching *Inspector Gadget* and *The Smurfs*.

Bedtime is also one of my favorite early memories because I learned to pray by listening to Momma as she recited the Lord's Prayer before bed. I didn't have my own room at Momma's, but I had the pleasure of sleeping between Momma and Grandpa or sleeping in bed with one of my aunts. They always made room for me. They didn't seem to mind the way my small frame took up more than half the size of the bed, so they had to skootch over to the very edge of the mattress. Nor did they mind that I sometimes hogged more than my share of the bed covers.

One night when I was sick, I cuddled under the weight of one of Momma's homemade patchwork quilts, as she nursed me back to health. She said, "Lay down and get some rest. The doctor says you have pneumonia." Loving the extra attention from Momma, I acted sicker than I actually was. As she removed the thermometer from under my tongue and placed the back of her hand on my forehead, she said, "You're 103 degrees." When I was sick, she fed me Sprite, saltine crackers, and chicken noodle soup.

During my childhood years, my nose frequently bled—whether it was summer, spring, or fall. My nose bled when I awoke in the morning, sometimes before I went to bed, and at times while I was playing outside. When it happened, Momma would quickly run a face towel under cold water, fold it neatly, and place it on my forehead. She'd say, "Get in the bed and rest." Then she'd prop three or four pillows, so I could sit up while I recovered. She always seemed ready with an ointment or a home remedy to rush to my aid with the resolve to help me feel better. She gave me the blueprint for how to love others when I became an adult and had my own family.

* * *

Momma and Grandpa's land consisted of wide-open fields, dandelions, honeysuckle blossoms, pecan trees, and blackberry bushes. My cousins and I ran around playing hide-and-seek, tag, and red rover. Once, six of us were playing football, and it was the only time in my life when I got to truly play. Whenever it rained, we sat in the dirt and made mud pies, as if we were eating them for real. We drank cool water from the garden hose and strutted down the center of Apple Street as if we owned the road. In the summer days when our bodies were dusty and damp from playing in the sweltering heat all day, my cousins and I took turns cooling off in front of a box fan or the living room window AC unit.

About a mile up the road in either direction were different versions of old-timey country stores. One was made of old barn wood, with a large front porch and rickety steps. It looked as if it had been built in the 1800s, and if I had been born a half-century earlier, I would have been shopping there for a white family instead of for myself.

But in the 1980s, we filled our lunch-sized brown paper bags with a hundred pieces of candy for a dollar. We stuffed the creases of our arms with Doritos, Dr. Pepper, and banana-flavored Laffy Taffy. I loved coming home and pouring my candy on the coffee table, looking at my idea of a pot of gold. It was a time in my life when I lived freely, without fear of the unknown. Truly carefree, I had no menacing thoughts of someone harming me, and no thoughts of harming myself. I awoke each day to a new day and harbored no fears of the future. Most of all, I did not hunger for affection. On Sundays, Momma's TV was always tuned in to Apostle Frederick K.C. Price's sermons while we dressed for church. She believed in God and being good to people. She said, "Regardless of how people treat you, you treat them right. God will repay you." She taught me to serve people with a pure heart.

Now in retrospect, Momma's voice becomes shaky and stressed when she recounts the mental and emotional anguish she endured when Katrina, who often acted impulsively and irrationally, would show up at Momma's house unexpectedly in a fit of rage. "She wanted to control everything. She'd come over here cussing and talking to me like I was nothing. It hurts me to think about it. She put me through so much. All I wanted to do was take care of you the best I knew how. I don't know what kind of life she had, but you could tell she was going through some stuff."

One of my uncles stated, "Your mother did things that other people just didn't do. She was out of control, violent, and crazy. She would show up at the house screaming for no reason, threatening to hurt somebody." But why? I asked my aunts if anyone had cause to provoke her. They always replied with a resounding, "No."

Aunt Yolanda said, "Honey, she didn't just get crazy, she's been crazy since the beginning. Even back in high school, she walked around looking for ways to cause trouble. People knew to stay away from her 'cause she was off." *Off* being a synonym for mentally challenged, crazy, unhinged, weird. Aunt Yolanda continued, "Everybody who knows her knows she's got problems."

There were aspects of my childhood at Momma's house in Pine Bluff that were absolutely idyllic, and I wouldn't trade those early memories for the world. However, there was a lot more that was going on in the adult world that I couldn't yet perceive when viewing the world through a child's eyes. It's only after I matured and came into my own that I was able to newly reflect on the dysfunction I witnessed in my maternal and paternal lineage. Silence on both sides of my family set a precedent for the rest of my life. Questions lingered in the air like musk: who abused who, why, and for how long?

Many of Momma's children were touched by addiction, mental health challenges, or sexual abuse. To my knowledge, no one in Momma's family spoke about these violations of body and soul. Without the chance to shed light on these tribulations by addressing them squarely and legitimately, they became family secrets which resulted in internalized shame, festering resentment, and unspoken brokenness. Instead of becoming survivors of their addictions and abuse, my relatives fell victim to their unaddressed traumas.

The costly consequence for those I loved in my extended family was spiritual and emotional neglect which pierced their self-esteem, debased their lives' purpose, and fractured their ability to sustain healthy relationships. In those times in my life when I struggled most to understand my identity and my life's purpose, I often felt unseen by my closest relatives. My pleas for help were often met with indifference and detachment. In retrospect, I understand now that one cannot give to others what one has never possessed.

Momma raised her twelve children in the Arkansas house she and grandpa purchased in 1951. She said, "It was already old when we bought it." Decades past its best days, it was a dilapidated three-bedroom, one-story structure on a corner lot. In the early 2000s, the city tried but failed to convince Momma to move after they condemned it due to rotting walls, poor plumbing, paper-thin carpeting, and an infestation of critters. But Momma wouldn't relocate saying, "It's my home, and it's paid for. I'm not going anywhere."

The home's floorboards were so uneven in some areas of the house that we could touch the ceiling depending on where we stood. The living room windows remained closed and covered with plastic all year round, preventing any chance of the dry and musty smell which diffused throughout the house from escaping.

The infestation problem was so unchecked that cockroaches routinely crawled across the counters and along the walls in every room of the old house. For weekend overnight visits, my cousins and I pulled the bed covers over our bodies from head to toe so that cockroaches wouldn't crawl on our faces while we slept.The home was always a mess, cluttered throughout and reminiscent of the TV show *Hoarders*. Although, it wasn't as bad as that, and Momma wasn't as far gone as the people on the show.

Now as an adult with perfect hindsight, I see how Momma's broken-down house was a perfect metaphor for the brokenness within our family. Even while the house was occupied, it remained derelict and virtually uninhabitable over the years. Without any restoration planned for the future, how long the house would safely stand before collapsing in on itself was anyone's guess.

Like Momma's neglected house, how could her family unit thrive without the security of family members who have each other's back and each other's best interests in mind? Without anyone standing in as ethically moral and supportive pillars in each other's' lives, the mental and emotional well-being of my family members was constantly under threat of being destabilized. Habitually turning a blind eye to each other's suffering resulted in severe emotional neglect. The damage was done—fractures of permanent dysfunction beleaguered the lives of those I loved most.

CHAPTER 3

God's Plan

"Have I not commanded you? Be strong and courageous. Do not be afraid; do not be discouraged, for the LORD your God will be with you wherever you go."

~JOSHUA 1:9 (NIV)

My greatest childhood fear didn't involve spiders, snakes, darkness, or even dying. The thought that kept me up at night more than any other was, *What if I leave with Katrina, and she doesn't bring me back to Momma's? What if I'm kidnapped?* I didn't know my mother well, but God gives intuition for a reason.

Momma tried to calm me by saying, "Stop all that crying. You'll be back soon." But every time I was with Katrina for the weekend, "soon" felt like "never." I don't remember how or when the weekends with her began. All I know is that when they arrived, I always reacted the same way. Before Katrina picked me up for our weekend visits, I agonized over the forced reunion. My eyes would be puffy and swollen from crying, and tears would run down my neck and to my chest, as I used my shirt to wipe them.

When Katrina arrived, she didn't ask why I was crying or try to sooth me by holding me tight as a mother might. She offered no words of promise that I would feel better soon. No matter how many weekends I stayed with her, I never warmed up to her or her side of the family. She'd also married in the time since she and my father had separated. I endured forced embraces and kisses on the cheek from great-grandparents and great-aunts, uncles, and distant cousins. Her family spread throughout North Little Rock, Stuttgart, Wabbaseka, and Altheimer. Cornfields and cotton crops separated one small town from the next.

Each relative's home felt as uncomfortable as the next, and I didn't know why she was parading me around like this. The forced engagement was tormenting, and I only felt like myself when I was with Momma in Pine Bluff. The long, forty-minute drive back to her house as each weekend drew to a close felt like it took hours. All I wanted to do was return to Momma's haven as quickly as possible.

There were other times on these weekend excursions when Katrina would engage me as if to make a mother-daughter relationship materialize out of thin air. I remember one occasion when I was at Katrina's home watching *Road Runner* cartoons on the bedroom floor. Waving a Chick-O-Stick in the air, she beckoned me into the kitchen while saying, "Do you like these?" I didn't like peanut butter candy, but I nodded anyway, and she handed it to me. Holding a Polaroid camera in one hand, as she tickled me with the other, she directed, "Say CHEESE! Smile pretty for the camera." I laughed while holding the candy in the air, as the Polaroid picture which captured the moment was newly developing.

In the first few photos, I wore the simple, white, tank top and shorts I'd dressed in at Momma's house. My hair was wild and bushy, with strands of unmanageable hair sticking up and away from my plaits. I looked like a kid fresh off the playground after a raucous game of tag. Modeling for her helped me to forget how uncomfortable and inhibited I'd felt only moments before. I looked like a kid whose big, beautiful, brown eyes and wide smile expressed joy. Pictures never lie, right?

She then said, "Sit down so I can do your hair." Obediently, I sat on the floor with my legs crisscrossed watching *I Dream of Jeannie,* as she greased my scalp, brushed my baby hairs down the side of my face, and combed my hair into two pigtails. Lastly, she added white bows at the top of each pigtail. She left the room for a moment and returned with a new dress, a white petticoat, matching white lace-trimmed socks, and black patent leather shoes. She instructed, "Change clothes, so I can see how you look."

I wondered why I had to put on fancy clothes on a Saturday. Once I had everything on, she said, "Stand in front of the mirror. SAY CHEESE!" I recall standing directly in front of the floor-length mirror giggling with my head tossed back, twisting and turning, with my hands confidently placed on my hips. I loved my new clothes. The peach, layered, ruffle dress had cinched cap sleeves. Each weekend when I visited, she let me wear and try on new clothes but made me take them off when our time together ended. She bluntly said, "You ain't taking those clothes over there. Put your old clothes on."

When I was about the age of six, Momma roused me from my sleep one morning by saying, "Get up. Get dressed." She rushed from room to room the way people do when their alarms don't wake them up on time. She grabbed all of my clothing and wrapped it in tightly folded newspaper. She mumbled to herself, and something didn't feel right. Soon, we were on the way to the courthouse. When we arrived, the court staff directed Momma and me to a small room that was empty except for a brown rectangular table and five chairs. The white walls, shiny white linoleum floors, and white ceiling tiles stood out. The unfamiliarity and starkness of the courtroom made me afraid.

Holding Momma's hand, I prayed, God, please help me. The judge who presided was a white man in his fifties with shiny, slick, brown hair. When he entered the room,

I stared at him anxiously and waited for him to say something, anything. While I glanced at the adults and again at my belongings wrapped like a gift, Momma looked straight ahead somewhat in a daze. The judge brandished a polite, professional smile as he said, "Unfortunately, she has to return to her mother. All the conditions set by the court have been met. I'll allow her to go home with you one last time. I've also written in my order that she is to visit you on weekends and school breaks."

Momma had openly discussed the fact that Katrina was my real mother, but at such a young age, I didn't think much about it. I never considered her to be anything more than a lady I spent weekends with sometimes. I hadn't considered the possibility that I'd ever have to live with her full-time.

Katrina had used the pictures she'd taken to influence the judge's ruling regarding her fitness and ability to be a responsible parent. At the time, I thought Katrina and I were having fun. I thought we were getting to know each other. My innocence and naïveté had helped her to make a case against Momma. I've rewound the scene a hundred times in my head, going back to those moments in front of the mirror. Later blaming myself, I thought, Why did I have to smile so big? Did I have to show all my teeth? Years later, my mother admitted she would pick me up and take pictures to show the judge how poor and dirty I looked. "You didn't have a damn thing living in that house, and now look at you." Each time she spoke against Momma, it felt like darts hitting the center of my chest.

During the six years I lived with Momma, the court had called it "kinship placement." This meant I was cared for by someone in the family other than my parents. Over the course of my childhood, Momma and other family members recall going to court five or six times before Katrina regained custody. They were always sure that each time would be the last. According to my aunts, the judge didn't require Katrina to complete mandatory parenting classes. There were also no psychological assessments to assess her mental fitness or readiness to parent. There was also no substance abuse testing.

I wish my six-year-old self could have interjected on our behalf in the conversation Momma had with the judge. Why didn't I state my reasons for wanting to stay with Momma? But I wasn't asked for my opinion, and there are good reasons for children's wishes not to be considered in the due process of law. It's been proven that children are typically not aware of what is in their best interest, so I had no sway in the outcome of the custody hearings.

Momma's eldest daughter, Aunt Gloria, often accompanied Momma to the courtroom. Aunt Gloria was a devout Pentecostal Christian like Reva's mom, Aunt Dorris. Gloria wore big curls, had a big smile, and an even bigger faith. She's the kind of woman who, when asked, *How are you*, says, "Blessed and highly favored." She gave me my first Bible, my first devotional, and my first book on Christian dating. Aunt Gloria remembered wanting to do more for me and desired to be a bigger part of my life, but she also feared Katrina's reaction. She told me she worried Katrina would hurt me in some way if she showed me too much affection.

Remembering the day Momma lost custody, Aunt Gloria said, "Your mother stood before the judge, and when he asked her if she felt ready to regain custody, she said 'yes.'" Knowing Katrina all too well, I picture her at the previous hearings impatiently glancing at her watch, chewing on gum, and acting as if she had somewhere better to be. Apparently, there were multiple court dates prior to the last court date, in which my mother, Katrina, stood before the judge and declared "no" when the judge pointedly asked her if she wanted to seek custody. I will never know who or what changed her mind, perhaps a conversation with Aunt Dorris. The day Katrina was awarded custody she arrived in the bleak courtroom arm-in-arm with Darryl, dressed in her Sunday best, with evidence of the steps she'd taken to be better suited to regain custody. I bet she thought, *I'll teach them.*

There are still many unanswered questions regarding my custody battle. To this day, no one I've asked has a full scope on what actually took place. The answers I yearn to know are forever cloaked in secrecy or obscurity. Why wouldn't the judge take her at face value and accept her first answer of "no" as her final answer?

Based on my understanding of custody battles at the time, court systems were biased towards mothers. Through conversations with social workers who have experience with cases such as mine, I've learned mothers were almost always awarded custody of their children, even in cases where evidence of child maltreatment and maternal substance abuse exists. The court's main goal in any case was reunification.

If the case were presented today, a parent seeking custody after being absent for the first six years of the child's life, wouldn't automatically be granted custody. Child protective services would most likely conduct home inspections and require familial interviews. The mother would very likely be subject to mandatory mental health assessments to evaluate her mental fitness, parenting classes to assess readiness, and a urinalysis to test for substance abuse, at the very least. None of these required standards were ever enforced in my custody case.

Character testimonials that could have otherwise shed light on Katrina's volatile personality and behavioral instability were also woefully lacking. Katrina's poor reputation in the family was well-established by that point. To my knowledge, none of Maurice's family members came forward to contest her in court. Such damning testimony could have made all the difference in the world. Momma didn't have a well-kept house or resources to buy expensive garments. But what she lacked in finances, she made up for in many other ways. I had in bulk what a six-year-old needed: food, shelter, clothing, safety—and most importantly, validation and love.

After my future was decided in court that day, the judge allowed me to return to Momma's house for a final goodbye. I sat down on the couch in the room where Aunt

Yolanda would always braid my hair. The very same room where Momma and I prayed on a regular basis. The room where I cried weekly until my body fell limp onto Momma's chest prior to my weekend visits with Katrina. That afternoon, after all was decided, Momma said as delicately as she could, "Katrina did everything. She found a house, got a job, and got married."

I still couldn't see how any of that mattered. Momma ended our talk by reassuring me, "God's got a plan for your life. And he is going to use you one day." Without saying anything, I looked up towards her face to detect if her words were true. Tears streamed down her cheeks as she held me. "You'll be back on the weekends. We have a court order, and your mom can't take you away from me," Momma pleaded with me. "Stop all that crying. She's on the way here. I don't want her to see you like this."

I tried to compose myself. While Momma held my hand and prayed for God to keep me safe, I prayed something different as I imagined Katrina changing her mind and turning her car around to head off in the opposite direction. God, please save me. Don't let her come.

CHAPTER 4

Nothing

Katrina arrived despite my prayers. She and her husband, Darryl, pulled into Momma's yard and honked the horn. Darryl was ten years her senior with dark skin, an oil-sheened Afro, and wooly sideburns. He said very little. He had a slim silhouette and donned tight-fitting dress shirts, wide-leg dress pants, and matching Stacy Adams shoes. One might mistake him for a member of a '70s quartet.

They stayed in the car, honked their horn again, and waited for me to come outside. When I got in their vehicle, Katrina introduced me to Darryl and told me to call him "Buster," a nickname he'd had since his days as a teenager. He called her "Kat." Once we were on the road, the strange feeling of being abducted by strangers nagged at me; it felt like I was suddenly inside a bad Lifetime movie. In that moment, I focused all of my attention on crying quietly, to not call attention to myself or cause her to notice me in her rearview mirror. My insides were kicking and screaming, triggering my fight-or-flight response, as we traveled farther and farther away from the place I called home.

Although I'd been to Katrina and Darryl's place before during prior weekend visits, this time it felt like the first time, in that I noticed things anew: the siding on the house, the chain-link fence running the perimeter of their yard, and the sparse grass. A snarling, white, pit bull stood on all four legs in the backyard. His bark sounded more like wailing, as he yanked on the metal chain. Why hadn't I noticed this dog before? Where did he come from? Most likely, the dog had been there previously, but until that day I hadn't been engrossed with any of the details which I now saw with microscopic vision.

Walking through her front door and into the living room, Katrina ordered, without so much as looking in my direction, "Take off your clothes and go to bed." She spoke as if I were an inmate, and she were a correctional officer. Puzzled and alone in my discomfort, I looked through the nearest window to verify that it was not yet nightfall. I thought, *Why are we going to sleep at this hour?*

At Momma's house, bedtime didn't come until after dinner and the evening news. The twin bed where I had previously slept now contained boxes, bags, and piles of clothes. Taking stock of the layout of the rooms in Katrina's house, I tried to find a place to rest. I didn't understand why they hadn't prepared a place for me to sleep. Had they been surprised by the verdict? Katrina turned around and noticed the confused look on my face. I was in shock, and everything about that first day felt oddly new.

"Go in the bathroom," she ordered.

I complied, but even after shuffling into the bathroom, it took a few seconds for me to come to my senses. The laminated walls, bathtub, and toilet were all institutionally clean. Why hadn't I noticed this before? Momma's house lacked a daily cleaning routine, which was made obvious by the often-stained toilet, overfilled trashcan, and the brownish gunk which perennially rimmed the dirty bathtub. Standing on the cold linoleum floor, I could barely move a muscle as I tried to make sense of all that had happened in the last few days. I wanted to cry, but I stifled all of my feelings for fear she would hear me.

That night, I slept on the couch which was next to Katrina and Darryl's bed. With little to no privacy, I pulled a thin sheet up to my face. I tried praying silently, but my insecurities and fears felt out of God's reach. *God, if you're listening, I'm so scared. Please keep me safe and keep your angels around me. In Jesus' name, I pray. Amen.* To soothe myself, I visualized angels surrounding me. They were floating in the air with large wings at least six-feet tall. I didn't sleep that night, or many of the nights that followed.

I tried to envision Katrina as my full-time mom. Would she be up to embracing all the full-time responsibilities? I tried to picture her registering me for school, watching me as I played outdoors, listening to me breathe as I slept, hugging me if I awoke with night terrors. She would have to help me hold my head back if my nose bled and then place a cold towel on my forehead as Momma had. Would she, though? When I arrived at Katrina's house, I didn't yet have an adult's perspective on what it was like for Katrina to have just been awarded custody. Maybe she didn't know what to do—so, with gross neglect, she did nothing. I didn't have the presence of mind then that I do now. While I didn't need her to be the perfect mom, I needed her to have the presence of mind to do me no harm. Sadly, time would reveal her true nature. As children, we don't often imagine our parents as still growing or still learning. It's painfully obvious to me now that she had a lot to learn as a twenty-four-year-old, just as many of us do in our twenties.

After moving in with Katrina, I quickly learned that I needed to walk on eggshells or risk her berating me for any reason she found plausible. Something as simple as tiptoeing to the kitchen to quench my thirst with a glass of water felt like stepping into a minefield. I walked as delicately as possible, hoping not to alert her. Trying to be quiet and unnoticed became a way of life for me. I wonder now if it's because I wanted the power to disappear.

Within days of moving into Katrina's house, I realized I had another problem. I knew her name but found myself reluctant to call her Mom. She didn't clarify if I should call her "Momma" or "Mommy," and I didn't ask. This omission added to the already tense awkwardness between us. I certainly didn't view her as my mother, so, with nothing to call her, I called her nothing. When asking permission to watch cartoons, I didn't bother with, "Mommy, may I watch cartoons?" Instead, I said, "May I watch cartoons?" This aloof communication style lasted for years.

Within a few weeks of my move there, she introduced me to Anthony, who was my ten-year-old brother. He lived with Aunt Dorris and Reva in North Little Rock for the early part of his life, but he visited us occasionally. The atmosphere in the home was less tense when he visited. A rambunctious kid, confident in his skin, he often skipped and trotted from room to room. His conversations with Katrina were peppered with laughter and easy banter. As I pressed my ear against the living room wall, eavesdropping, they sounded like best friends. When observing them together, her voice was gentle and playful, when she looked his way. Feeling already out of my element, seeing that they apparently spoke the same language made me feel terrible. They laughed together in rooms where my invite got misplaced.

At bedtime, with no additional beds in the home, Anthony and I were told to share the couch in Katrina's bedroom. I was dismayed by this situation, and I hoped to hear Anthony volunteer to sleep elsewhere. Instead, he said, "I'll sleep on this end and you can sleep on that end of the couch." With his long legs pressed against mine like the seal on a Ziploc bag, he made an already uncomfortable sleeping arrangement significantly worse. I had shared sleeping space at Momma's too, but Momma would never make me sleep next to someone I hardly knew. She'd put me in bed with her.

As time passed, things never got less awkward between us. Katrina and I never fell into easy step with each other. Being forced to cohabitate with Katrina and Darryl felt nothing like joining a family unit. I don't recall having a single meal with Katrina and Darryl at the same time and in the same room. I felt more like a foster kid with foster parents who might remark, "We don't like kids." It's very possible Katrina didn't know how to create a family, having no experience for what it actually felt like herself.

At first, Katrina obeyed the court order and allowed visits to Momma's on the weekends. But over time, Katrina got lax and didn't stick to the letter of the law. She arbitrarily reduced my visitation rights from every weekend to every other weekend, and shortly after that, my visits to Momma's became less and less frequent. Eventually, I visited Momma for only a week or two during the summer. Katrina made other plans for my weekends and kept us busy. We cleaned the house, pressed our hair, and visited people I didn't know. Each day blurred into the next. I didn't keep close track of when the weekends designated for Momma's arrived, and I eventually failed to notice when we missed a visit. Over time, there was a huge emotional toll which negatively impacted my sense of belonging. When I didn't hear from Momma or see my extended family, I convinced myself they'd forgotten about me. While it was Katrina who was restricting their access to me, I made myself believe I no longer mattered to them. To some weird degree, my distorted way of rationalizing their absence in my life helped me to suppress the emotional pain of missing them.

Within two years of gaining custody, as if to wag her finger at Momma and say "na-na na-na boo boo," Katrina bragged, "We're moving to Little Rock. I don't give a damn what the judge says. You ain't going there every weekend. If they want to see you, they can take my ass back to court." She knew Momma had never learned to drive and couldn't afford attorney's fees. My aunts and uncles also had busy lives of their own, and going out of their way to check on my welfare was most likely a burden. As an adult, I later learned they worried about what Katrina might do if they tried to visit, call, or send gifts. Katrina could prove to be very vindictive, and they said, "We didn't want her to hurt you."

My extended family members stated that they had distanced themselves for my protection.During that time of growing up feeling all alone, I felt betrayed and exceptionally forgotten. In my deep loneliness, I often fantasized about Momma coming to my rescue, with my Aunt Yolanda banging her fist on Katrina's door, and the both of them demanding to see my face. They would then help me to pack my bags, and I would be safely taken away. But no matter how often I daydreamed of their heroic rescue, I was only met with a wall of silence. A part of God's plan must have included showing me what love was by having me experience first-hand all that it wasn't.

CHAPTER 5

The 8ᵗʰ Year

"At best the family teaches the finest things human beings can learn from one another generosity and love. But it is also, all too often, where we learn nasty things like hate, rage and shame."

~BARBARA EHRENREICH

We initially moved into a first-floor apartment in a walnut brick building that was forty-five minutes from Pine Bluff. It was located in a high-traffic, high-crime area. Anthony moved in as well. Darryl was absent during this relocation, but he did join us a year later when we relocated again to a new home. I slowly began to accept my new normal and the reality of my day-to-day, which became more bleak while we lived in the apartment.

Katrina often made a point of making me feel out of place in my new home.

One afternoon, while she entertained a girlfriend, I looked around my room for toys or anything that was water-safe. There were no age-appropriate toys or girly things at Katrina's house. I missed My Little Pony, Barbie dolls, and the Lite-Brite set that were available to me at Momma's. Without the traditional bath toys I'd had at Momma's house, I eyed a small stuffed rabbit sitting against the pillows on my bed. Talking, playing, and singing while in the tub, I dunked the rabbit in the water in an effort to re-create bath time at Momma's. Afterwards, with my small hands and bath towel, I twisted the rabbit and wrung out as much water as possible before placing it back on the bed.

A couple of hours later, Katrina yelled my name. When I met her in my room, she held the rabbit in front of her like a specimen. "Why is it wet?"

Diverting eye contact, I said, "I wanted to have something to play with while bathing."

"Your stupid ass should know better!" she responded. "I paid a lot of money for this rabbit. It stays on the bed!" She went into her room, retrieved a belt, and whooped me as I lay face down, my body tense on the bed. "You're so damn stupid you don't even know stuffed animals don't belong in water." When she returned to her friend, she said loudly to ensure I was in earshot and to further embarrass me, "Ain't she a dummy?" I couldn't tell whether her friend responded. Had I really done something that awful? For the rest of the night, I consoled myself in my room.

Most of my childhood is a blur, consisting of gaping holes I am still unable to fill. But I vividly remember being eight. That's when some parts of who I am today began— and it's when other parts of me ended. Prior to the wet rabbit incident, I don't remember Katrina ever hitting me. In Little Rock, life drifted in the wrong direction and physical abuse from Katrina became more commonplace. I became her punching bag, and I felt uncomfortable and grew afraid more often than not. After one of her beatings, she would often gossip to her friends on the phone about the stupid things I'd done. She always spoke loudly, so I could hear her voice as it trailed into my room.

After the rabbit incident, she held my shame over my head for days, weeks, and months afterward. I was living under a dark cloud of verbal abuse which did not dissipate. She'd say, "You think you're so smart, but you're not. You're a fucking idiot. Look what you did with that rabbit."

In another incident a few weeks later, after school, I eyed an unopened box of Little Debbie Swiss Rolls and ate one. The chocolate, cream-filled rolls were so light and delicious. I licked the packaging and used my fingers to pick up fallen pieces of the flaky chocolate exterior. I could eat them all day. They were one of my favorite snacks, so when I saw the box of treats on our counter, I couldn't help but indulge myself. When Katrina arrived home, she called Anthony and me downstairs into the kitchen.

Looking inside the box, she said, "Who ate a Swiss Roll?"

I said, almost as an automatic reflex, "I don't know."

Looking at both of us again, she said, "*Who* ate the Swiss Roll?"

Anthony shrugged his shoulders in response. He then looked at me, and mouthed the words, "*Tell her!*"

I stubbornly defended myself and said again, "I didn't do it." No matter how many times she interrogated me, I lied. The more I denied her accusation, the more infuriated she became. She stomped out of the room in order to retrieve the thick leather belt she would beat both of us with that afternoon. "When I come back downstairs, somebody better fess up. Spare the rod, spoil the child."

Upon her return, with her whipping belt in hand, she said to Anthony and me, "Both of you, pull down your pants and bend over." Yelling as she swung the belt, she whipped Anthony first striking him all along his lower back and butt, as she said, "Did you eat it? Tell the truth!" Then she looked at me. "If you ate it, you better say something. Are you going to let him keep getting beaten?" She stopped hitting him after twenty or thirty lashes. The severity of her punishment was so disproportionate to the crime. I watched in guilty agony as Anthony jumped and yelped reacting to the pain of each whip. I tried to think of how I could stop her corporal punishment, but I didn't have the courage to tell the truth.

After beating Anthony, she became immediately remorseful. "Anthony, I'm sorry I had to whoop you. I know who ate the cake." She pointed her finger at me while holding the belt in the other hand. "I know you did it. You're evil. Why would you make me whoop him? You ain't nothing but a liar." Katrina justified her fits of rage by rationalizing that my lies fueled her anger. When in fact, her chronic anger was at the root cause of my habitual lying.

Anthony and I never knew which of our petty offenses would cause Katrina to fly off the handle next. In hindsight, it appears to me that she wanted to pit one sibling against the other. After beating us both, she would endear herself to him to the same degree that she would vilify me. Her behavior was very polarizing, and it gave Anthony a reason to see me as the indirect cause of the cherry-colored bruises along his arms and legs. No matter what I said or did, my very existence seemed to antagonize her...

CHAPTER 6

The Before and After

My year in third grade began with a list of rules. If you were also a latchkey kid growing up, these rules might also have applied to you:

1. *Lock the door when you get home.*

2. *Don't answer the phone or door for anyone.*

3. *Don't tell anyone you're home alone.*

4. *Don't make any noise.*

5. *Don't talk to strangers.*

But one afternoon upon coming home, I was unexpectedly besieged, despite having followed the perceived rules. After getting off the school bus for the short walk

home, I used my door key like any other day. As I opened
the door, my brother immediately followed in behind me,
seemingly appearing out of nowhere.

He jumped in front of me, and leveled his gaze on
me like a hawk eyeing prey. He asked, "Have you started your period yet?" Being only eight, I didn't know
what he meant.

I said "no" and avoided eye contact, unsure of what
to do or how to act in the present moment. As he slung his
backpack onto the couch beside him, he responded, "You
can't get pregnant. You haven't had a period yet."

I thought, Period? I don't know what he's talking about.
I couldn't help but wonder where he'd learned about girls'
periods. Wearing thick, black-framed bifocals, he glared
in my direction and said, "We don't have a lot of time.
Take off your pants and lay on the couch." I was puzzled
by my brother's behavior but found myself obediently un-
dressing as he'd asked. I again avoided eye contact while
he watched me and thought to myself, *Is he serious?* In the
time leading up to this afternoon, Anthony and I more
or less tolerated each other as siblings, although we felt
no particular warmth towards one another. Still, I found
myself looking up to him. He had everything I wanted: a
close relationship with our mother, good grades, and the
affection of almost every person we met. People remarked
that he was smart, handsome, athletic, and respectful.
He seemed to already have won the adoration I was
so hungry for.

Unzipping his pants in haste, my twelve-year-old brother, who weighed more than twice as much as me, pulled down my underwear and began thrusting his penis between my thighs, touching the folds of my vagina. Lying there with my head pressed against the end of the couch, I thought, *What is he doing? Why is he on top of me? Why?* But I didn't say anything. He kept quiet as well. I remember disassociating from my immediate surroundings, detaching from the physical reality of what was happening, like an out of body experience. I remember wondering if Katrina and Anthony had conspired against me. After a few minutes, he finished, stood up, and zipped up his jeans. As I collected myself and pulled my panties back up around my waist, I felt the wetness he posited between my thighs. Within seconds of me standing up to straighten my clothes, I heard Katrina's keys jangling just outside the front door. As she walked in, I froze. Unable to process what had just happened, I looked towards her but couldn't find the words to speak. Her hands were full of grocery bags, and she sounded unusually upbeat when she said, "Hey, what are y'all doing?"

We didn't answer, so she asked Anthony, "What'd you do today?" Her voice sounded animated, like it belonged to a mother on TV. I found myself thinking, Why is she in *such* a good mood? Anthony answered for the both of us. "Nothing. We're about to do homework."

As Katrina and he continued to talk about his day, I ducked out of sight and headed upstairs. I went into the bathroom, and after using a washcloth to wipe myself clean, I hid my underwear in the bottom of the laundry basket.

I had known Anthony as my brother for a period of about two years prior to the assault. The moment he touched me in that way, he became a stranger, and I no longer felt safe around my older brother. Now an adult, the memory of sexual violation continues to haunt me because it represents for me the end of my childhood. Anthony made me aware of my body in a way that I hadn't been until that day. He touched me in ways I didn't want, need, or ask for. My early life was now split into two halves: before the sexual assault and afterwards.

Before, I hadn't so much as looked at my vagina or given thought to how the area between my legs might give someone pleasure. I didn't know anything about boys' sexual urges. I hadn't heard the word "period." After Anthony raped me, and my vagina no longer belonged to me. I felt useless, dirty, and deformed. I understood for the first time that my body could be taken hostage at any moment for the satisfaction of another. Anthony's actions made me wonder if anyone else would ever want my vagina or touch my vagina in the same way. I even found myself ruminating obsessively, running a mental checklist of any other suspicious physical encounters I had with uncles and even Maurice. I wondered if they had touched me before, and my brain just couldn't recall the moment of violation.

The *before* included many days when I could recall being happy with Momma and my family in Pine Bluff.

After the inappropriate touching, nothing mattered, and I lost sight of what it meant to enjoy the simple things in life. I forgot how it felt to feel safe without anxiety or debilitating self-consciousness. Having no one to confide in, I felt sure no one cared. If they did, why had they left me in the hands of a hateful woman and her deviant son? I felt far from the only family I knew, and I considered everyone else I encountered to be a stranger. Without family, I felt I had nothing, and I told myself no one was coming to rescue me.

When I think back to that day, I remember it as one of the few days Katrina was in a good mood. I can't help but feel suspicious of that. On the day my own brother violated my body, she came home exceptionally happy. Why so? Maybe I should have told her right then, confronted her somehow. Maybe she would have sent me back to Momma or taken some other course of action that could have protected me or shielded me. But if I shared the truth of what took place, I'm not entirely sure she would have believed me. Why would she when she'd accused me on multiple occasions of being a liar? It does me no good to think my own mother would orchestrate something so heinous. But when I look back at all the other events that occurred then, and in the years following, I can't help but scrutinize her intentions.

I stayed in my room for the remainder of that night. Part of me wanted to hide from Katrina and Anthony, and the other part of me didn't know how to exist in the world anymore. I tried to move through life with a sense of normalcy in the weeks, months, and years afterwards, at times questioning the wrongfulness of what happened. But in the wake of the sexual abuse, I felt naked in Anthony's presence, and when we were in the same room, I avoided him. For years, I convinced myself I had consented because I didn't cry, say "no," or put up a fight. I blamed myself for lacking the courage to refuse or defend myself. I spent a total of about six years in the same home with Anthony. After Anthony graduated from high school, he was admitted to the Naval Academy. Thankfully, we did not keep in touch.

As time passed, I assumed *all* boys were like my brother. I viewed my heterosexual relationships through a distorted lens, stemming from my sexual abuse. Even when the males I got to know didn't want or ask for sex, I offered and sometimes pressured them into having sex with me. I assumed that if I gave them my body, they would like and accept me. I assumed if I gave my body willingly, at least I could be in control of the moment. The little girl in me yearned to have agency over my body— I said *yes* to lovers who desired my body to avoid someone from ignoring my *no*.

Years later, when memories of the assault came to mind, I'd wonder if I was Anthony's only victim, or if he went on to assault others. I asked myself what would become of a boy who, at the age, of twelve had molested his sister? As a child himself, maybe he didn't understand inappropriate touch or that he had committed an act of incest. Did he grow up to become one of those men you see on Dateline who stalked unsuspecting women? Or was he now the kind of man who used his power and influence to sexually intimidate or harass vulnerable women? And, if so, would his crimes eventually catch up with him?

CHAPTER 7

Boys Will Be...

A year after my incestual sexual assault at the age of eight, Anthony and I were ironically strange bedfellows, in that we still shared time together under the same roof. While I never felt the same way about my body ever again, time passed and blunted the memory of the violation. Perhaps I shouldn't have ever buried or kept secret the depravity of what happened that afternoon. But as time marched on, I acclimated to the point where I no longer actively avoided Anthony. One day we were home alone with two of his friends, and he suddenly asked the other boys, "You wanna hump my sister?"

The boys looked in my direction, as I sat unassumingly on the couch in the living room. One boy, Shawn, had a husky build. He wore baggy pants that bunched around his ankles. He was about the same age as Anthony.

Whenever I saw him, he looked awkward and disheveled, as if he wasn't comfortable with his oversized body. He looked like a kid who played football, snored, and ate too much junk food. The other boy, named Travis, was my age and had braces and lips so big they looked swollen. He and I would later attend the same high school, but he didn't remember me. Travis dressed nicely, always wearing creased jeans and tucked-in shirts. Adults called them both "good boys."

That day, while we were at home without Katrina or Darryl to put a stop to things, the three boys took turns, still fully clothed, groping me underneath my shirt, dry humping me, and touching my rear end. Being nine years old at the time, I remember treating it like a game. I said, "Where do you want me?" I remember one of the boys telling me to stand, and then he used a hand to bend me over; afterwards he placed both of his hands on the sides of my waist. Still fully clothed, he proceeded to pull and push my body back and forth against his genitals as fast as he could. It's hard for me to remember my exact response, but I recall thinking, *This is what boys do.* I remember reacting to the ordeal as if it were an ordinary game of tag. I came to expect that Anthony and other boys would go on to do the same.

Following the second occurrence of sexual molestation and abuse, I began to suffer from signs of post-traumatic stress that school year. I recall having lapses in my short-term memory and an inability to focus on even the smallest tasks for any stretch of time. I forgot so many details, including the names of my classmates and teachers. To this day, there are large gaps in my memory when I try and actively recall that time during my troubled childhood. While the details of my second sexual molestation were still in my mind, the unspeakable transgressions forever colored the way I viewed my physical body and my self-worth.

CHAPTER 8

The Making of a Bully

After we leave this world, all we have is our legacy. How we spent our time, but more so, how we treated others.

~ME

At school, my emotions were all over the place. I was either in an emotionally comatose state, or I was emotionally burning up like an inferno. While in third grade, the same year as my molestation, when the kids in class eagerly raised their hands to answer the teacher's questions, I cowered for fear I would be called to the front of the class or singled out. I didn't retain much—if any—of the lessons or class activities, and I struggled with most tests and quizzes.

During lunch, I sat with everyone but avoided conversing with other children. I didn't have anything to add to their discussions. How could I relate? Boys called me silly names like "Big Dummy," "Moose," or "African Booty Scratcher." In response to the name-calling, I used my hands as weapons and challenged them to fight me by saying, "I dare you to hit me."

While sitting in the back of the school bus, a kid named, Robert, and a few of his friends were yelling and making fun of me. I'll never forget his haircut because the hi-top fade he wore reminded me of *Gumby Kids*, as they laughed and pointed in my direction. With the palm of my hand, I slapped him on the side of his head about three or four times. Robert stood up, and that's when it hit me: *this kid could hurt me if he wanted to.* Calmly, he said, "My mom taught me to never hit girls." He defended himself against my hits by placing me in a headlock and holding me in a bent, awkward position. The boys seated near us yelled for him to let me go, but he wouldn't budge. Other kids laughed, while I stood bent between his arm and side. I murmured, "I'm going to kill you." But I smiled on the inside even as my head faced the emergency exit, and my butt faced everyone else. I couldn't have shared it with him, but I respected Robert for not hitting me.

Within the same year, the teacher assigned one of my classmates the task of monitoring the class while she attended to a matter in the hallway. She told Rachel, a white girl with a dark, chocolate bob and under-eye freckles, to take down the names of anyone who talked or got out of their seat. As soon as the teacher shut the door, I started talking to the kids at my table. Rachel walked to the front of the class and said, "I'm telling Ms. Schmidt. No one's allowed to talk." When the teacher returned, she asked Rachel if anyone misbehaved. Rachel gave her my name. Ms. Schmidt wrote my name on the chalkboard with a check beside it. After three strikes, she would send a note home to our parents describing our bad conduct.

Once the bell rang at the end of the day, I cornered Rachel and pushed her against the wall. She fell, and I jumped on top of her. I began choking her and yelling, "I hate you! I'm going to kill you! I wish you would die!" After the words fell from my lips, I felt remorseful and began to cry. Rachel looked at me and said, "Kids can't kill kids." I removed my hands from her neck, as we both stood up to leave. She rubbed the area on her neck. We both cried, and I apologized. Afterwards, I ran faster than usual to get on the school bus and hide, praying I wouldn't get caught or be reprimanded for my bad behavior. Minutes later, two teachers ran outside. I could hear them asking if anyone saw me get on the bus. They stepped onto the bus but luckily didn't walk down the aisle to find me hiding between the seats.

I've often thought about how I bullied Rachel. I wonder if I caused her to fear or hate black people. I wonder if that moment haunted her. What if I am cemented in her mind as her first bully? What if Rachel hated school because of me? The terrified look in her eyes has stayed with me. She lay on the ground defenseless but strong in her belief that I couldn't hurt her. Her confidence in that moment provided the pause I needed to recognize that she didn't deserve my anger. When I read about children being bullied and committing suicide, I sometimes think of what I did to Rachel.

CHAPTER 9

Academically Speaking

As third grade came to a close, about a month before summer break, my homeroom teacher Ms. Schmidt called Katrina for a parent-teacher conference. She said I might not be able to advance to the fourth grade with the rest of my classmates because I failed math. They set a date for the following week at 4:00 p.m. Between Friday, when the teacher called, and the conference the following week, I dreaded going home each day, unsure of whether my teacher would call again with more bad news.

On the day of the conference, I studied Katrina's mannerisms. She didn't like white people, and she didn't like anyone (especially another woman) who she perceived to be in a position of higher authority. In such situations, Katrina always responded with *uh-huhs* and *yeahs*, as if the teacher had lied about my grades. Ms. Schmidt was in her early thirties and sported long dresses, pantyhose, and black kitten heels. Her hair was always perfectly coifed and the pink lip gloss she wore flattered her face. She reminded me of a woman from the 1960s who wore an apron and heels, as she prepared dinner for her family.

At the conference, Ms. Schmidt held up charts, tests, and even the gradebook where she kept track of my low homework grades and poor test scores. Ms. Schmidt spoke in a soft and gentle tone, maintaining eye contact with Katrina while explaining the reasons for her concern. As I sat there listening to my teacher, a barrage of self-critical thoughts ran through my mind. She's right—I should fail. I don't know how to do fractions or decimals. In fact, I'd developed a bad cheating habit, and I looked covertly at my neighbor's test any chance I could get.

I felt equally resentful of Katrina's performance, as I observed her putting on airs, acting as if she truly cared about my failing grades. Not once had she offered to help with homework. But when report cards arrived, she compared my mediocre grades to Anthony's good grades. His achievements in school gave her bragging rights with friends and family. I'd overheard her on the phone countless times going on and on about Anthony making honor roll and saying all his teachers liked him. Never once did she ever compliment me with words of praise or encouragement.

As the parent-teacher conference concluded, Ms. Schmidt asked my mother her opinion about either enrolling me in summer school or having me repeat third grade.

Katrina replied curtly, "No, she will not be held back, and she ain't going to no summer school."

Ms. Schmidt replied, "Well, you're her parent, and it's your decision. Maybe a new teacher will be good for her, but I recommend a tutor."

I found it laughable that my teacher addressed Katrina as my "parent." If she only knew how little parenting was going on. If she only knew why I was struggling so much that I couldn't stay focused in class. Had she asked, I might have told her everything.

CHAPTER 10

Why I Didn't Report

He replied, "Because you have so little faith. Truly I tell you, if you have faith as small as a mustard seed you can say to this mountain, 'Move from here to there,' and it will move. Nothing will be impossible for you."

~MATTHEW 17:20 (NIV)

A year after first relocating from Pine Bluff to Little Rock, we moved again. We were an emotionally bankrupt middle-class family—Katrina, Darryl, Anthony, and I. This time, we moved to a subdivision minutes from Little Rock Air Force Base. The neighborhood felt safer than the previous one. Our neighbors here were predominately white teachers, nurses, military members, and retirees.

We didn't have to worry about gang violence and bur-
glaries. The streets were clean and quiet. The lawns were
well-manicured with four-foot elephant ears, maple trees,
evergreens, and azaleas. Families walked their dogs,
jogged, and rode bikes.

During the years we all coexisted in the same house,
I never leaped out of my seat to greet or hug Katrina
and Darryl with open arms as they walked through the
door. I'd never run into the house after school, dropped
my backpack on the floor, and rushed to tell them about
my day. They'd also never wished me sweet dreams as
I settled underneath the covers at bedtime, and they
hadn't thought to walk me to the bus stop on my first
day of school.

During those years, my stepfather worked mid-shift
at Union Pacific Railroad, and he'd come home reeking
with an industrial-strength odor of earth and motor oil.
By this time, Katrina had opened her own shop after
graduating from the local beauty academy. She bragged
about the possibility of having a bustling business in our
small town. With a bit of weight in her voice, she said,
"I'm not just a hairdresser; I'm a cosmetologist."

The most basic but essential parts of normal family
dynamics were lost on us. Since first meeting one another,
we had neglected the conventional practices common to
most families, like eating together, having basic conversations, and spending time together in the same room.
Not once had I heard the words "I love you" from either
of my supposed parent figures. We cast long shadows

on each other in our home, in close proximity but never truly open or intimate with each other. To outsiders, we appeared as an average and normal family unit. I can't understand how we managed to live in a 1200-square-foot home while we skirted around each other, never truly acknowledging each other.

The lack of normal conversation in intimate enclosures such as during car rides made me often wish I could think of something and anything to say to the others to break the habitually deafening silence. In the eleven years I lived with Katrina, I developed a horrible nail-biting habit. Instead of learning how to exchange the most basic of pleasantries, in which I would have told her about my day, who I ate lunch with, or what was discussed in class, I compulsively bit my nails down to the quick. During car rides, I'd turn my face and gaze out the passenger-side window, my fingers never too far from my mouth. At nine years old, I was way past my early naïve attempts of trying to elicit a heartfelt mother-daughter moment with Katrina.

Our home looked identical to the rest of the homes in our neighborhood, totally nondescript. We fit in perfectly, or so it seemed to others who weren't privy to our dysfunctional family ties. Katrina painted the living room and hallway Pepto-Bismol pink, and she painted the other rooms pastel blue. My bedroom, however, remained contractor eggshell white. Nothing in the room was actually mine, and I felt like a stranger occupying another person's space. Katrina decorated my bedroom with more stuffed animals that didn't belong to me. The room looked picturesque but staged. I disliked the juvenile aesthetic of the pink and blue colors Katrina chose. Those colors didn't represent me, and they didn't quite fit her either, but appearances were important to her, and I had no choice in the matter. Lace doilies on glass tables and matching duck-shaped salt and pepper shakers completed the picture of our family's perfectly normal home.

Rather than our home being any sort of safe fortress for me, it was within the walls of this home where I endured not only sexual improprieties from Anthony but also incredibly tyrannical physical beat-downs from Katrina. One morning before school, I entered the kitchen to fix myself breakfast—plain Kellogg's Corn Flakes, which I detested. Opening the fridge, I noticed an unopened gallon of milk with a yellow cap. Assuming it must have been a different brand of milk than we usually purchased, I untwisted the top and smelled it. The label said "goats' milk." The strong, pungent, sour smell made me recoil. I placed the milk back in the fridge. I'd lost my appetite. As I waited for a bit to see if I could throw the cereal away, Katrina came into the kitchen.

I said, "There's something wrong with the milk. It smells sour." I imagined chunks had formed in the bottom of the carton, though I couldn't say for sure whether they had. Yanking the jug off the shelf, she placed it under her nose. "I just bought the damn milk!" She raised her hand, slapping my cheek and the side of my head.

My face stung. Knowing I didn't deserve such a harsh

rebuke, I held my hand to my cheek as if it were about to fall off, and I began to cry. I remember hating the way she made me feel.

Katrina looked at the milk label. "I didn't buy regular milk this time. This is goat's milk, and you're gonna drink it! Eat the damn cereal now!"

How she responded to me often depended on the given moment, her mercurial mood, and what type of weapon she had at her disposal. Sometimes she hit me with her hand, and other times, she used switches and belts. Once, she found a ceiling fan blade and whacked me with it. Another time she beat me with a plastic sword that belonged to a neighbor's child but had been left in our yard. Her actions were in response to my failing grades, my habitual lying, or simply because she'd had a bad day. A few times, but very few indeed, she apologized afterwards. The words "I'm sorry" would simply fall out of her mouth, but hearing this became meaningless to me because it was only a matter of time before she repeated her brutal behavior.

Another particularly abusive encounter I recall happened on a Saturday, when Katrina washed, blow-dried, and pressed my hair. She called me into the kitchen to sit me down on the stool. The hot comb was on the stove, heating up, while she greased my scalp.

As she parted my hair, taking small bits of hair near the nape of my neck and greasing my scalp with Sulfur 8, she said, "Your mammy tried to run me. She thought she was gonna tell me what to do and how to raise you.

I wasn't putting up with her shit. I bet you wish you still lived with her. You didn't have a damn thing when you were with her. If you wanna go back, I'll be glad to drop you off."

Without thinking to measure my response, I opened my mouth and said, "I love Momma. What'd she do wrong?" As soon as I spoke I suddenly knew I misspoke, and my body froze in anticipation of whatever barrage of insults would come next. As if right on cue, Katrina stopped pressing my hair, slammed the comb back onto the stove, and hit me over and over again with her open palm on the most tender, still-warm parts of my scalp. She slapped me so hard against the back of my head that I nearly fell off the chair. She was highly emotional and could hardly contain herself. She shouted, "If you wanna go live somewhere else, go ahead, you ungrateful ass."

Me revealing that I was close to anyone, especially Momma, led to Katrina's physical and emotional abuse. Her explosive rage came in unexpected moments, making it difficult to anticipate how to shield myself from the hits. What I know for certain is that the pain I endured had little to do with me. I did not cause the rage; therefore, I did not have within my arsenal the tools to extinguish the fire. Reflecting on this later, one thing I've learned is that having a tumultuous and abusive childhood is no excuse for continuing the cycle of abuse. All people, even victims of abuse, have choices.

Afterwards, Katrina left the kitchen and went into the bedroom and fell asleep. I opened the front door and ran across the street to a neighbor's house. I thought, *Maybe if I tell someone, they'll call the cops.* My feet moved before I had a chance to turn around or rethink my decision. I crossed the street and knocked on the door of the first house I saw. Panting, I rang the doorbell five, six, seven times. A tall, slender, white man with squinting and cautious eyes answered the door.

With one hand placed at his hip, he said, "May I help you?"

I knew the man served in the Air Force because of I'd seen him in uniform on my way to school on occasion. Out of breath, I said, "My mom is beating me. Can you please help me? I have to get away from her."

He replied, "Little girl, I don't know who you are, but my wife and I aren't getting involved."

I looked at him, crying and wailing. "Please help me, sir. She's sleeping. When she wakes up, she's going to beat me."

The man closed the door in my face, after which I raced home and sought refuge in my room. Within minutes, the neighbor whose aid I'd sought out was knocking on our door. Katrina answered and listened as the man regurgitated my statement regarding her, to her. Without expressing any compassion, he instead sounded angry about being roused from his complacency by some little kid. Rather than being of any help to me, he ensured I would be punished for my attempt to expose her. As I listened to him speak, and as I watched her nodding in agreement while mentioning something about me being a troubled child, I knew what was coming. Afterwards, she closed the door abruptly. That day, I received a beating I would not quickly forget, and she grounded me for two to three weeks. I could not watch TV, listen to music, or go outside. Sitting in the living room, taking slow drags from her cigarette, she said, "What goes on in this house, stays in this house."

CHAPTER 11

Luck

Taking steps across our front yard in the dew-drenched grass, I searched for a four-leaf clover. I waved my hand over dandelions, blades of grass, and various weeds. Naïve, I thought, *Maybe there's a small chance I will find one.* I've heard it said that superstition only comes true if you believe. In church, during youth Bible classes, they said, "All you have to do is believe, and God will answer your prayers." Minutes before I exited the house on my way to school, a rainbow spread halfway across the sky. I thought, *If rainbows are real, where's my pot of gold?* Each clover I selected only contained three leaves. After a few minutes, I held two three-leaf clovers and made my wish. Closing my eyes, I thought, *I wish the woman I know as my mother wouldn't hit me again.*

I asked myself a lot of questions. *What if, like the elusive four-leaf clover, happiness also eludes me? What if my faith in God doesn't change my circumstances? What am I left with?* At ten years old, I started a relationship with God and started praying to him like my life depended on it—I can't deal with this much longer, I beseeched him. Each morning while walking to the bus stop, I searched for the face of God or God's divinity in the clouds. I thought, *Please God, give me a sign.* My conversations with God were pointed. I didn't have time to beat around the bush. What's wrong with me? Why did you create me, if you hate me? Take my life if you're gonna make me live like this.

I had no plan to end my life, nor is that what I wanted. I'd never tried to kill myself up to that point. But I started having recurring dreams about running away, flying, and falling. I thought about my escape day and night. I needed God to know that as much as I believed and prayed, I didn't see an end to my misery. I was living in what felt like a never-ending nightmare. I needed God to know how much I hated my life, how much I would rather die than live another day being unloved. The walk to school gave me a sense of peace; a liberty to speak honestly to God.

There were countless nights when I awoke from night terrors, breathing heavily and holding my chest, I awoke alone, receiving no word of concern or kindness from a family member who worried for me. I couldn't shake the dread I felt each day when I came home from school. I felt captive living in a place where I had no one to confide in.

In one recurring dream, I found myself literally running from Katrina, who had friends, beasts, and a gang by her side. I was always outnumbered, and, in a lucid dream, I would run as fast as I could. Then, like an eagle, I flapped my arms until wide-brim angel wings grew from the expanse of my arms and gave me the lift off I needed to fly away from the source of my terrors. Every time I had this dream, I escaped successfully.

In other dreams, I fell from mountains, bridges, and skyscrapers. But somehow, I didn't crash, fall, or die. In most of my dreams, I had powers like the characters in the Marvel comics. I could think my way to safety because, in my dreams, whatever I envisioned happened. I had incredible agency, such as the power to levitate when the pain in my heart got too overwhelming. I could go from standing, to floating in the air seated in a lotus position. In my dreams, I could go anywhere as long as I had focus and determination. But I never had dreams that were happy, peaceful, or funny. I lived and slept in terror.

While I had few friends in school who were my age, I gravitated towards the kindness of well-intentioned adults. One such role model for me was the school librarian, Ms. McClure. She was a dark-skinned woman with bobbed hair, gold wire-framed glasses, and shiny lip gloss. She reminded me of the R&B singer, Lil' Mo. As soon as I saw her reading, I knew I liked her.

Every time I visited, her hands cupped a new book, and she was engrossed in reading. I never witnessed her engaged in actual library work, so I felt uninhibited about

interrupting her and introducing myself. As we got better acquainted, I trusted her because no matter when I
visited, she'd ask me to have a seat and would say with
genuine interest, "So, how's your day?" She also shared
details about herself and about the books she read. She
listened so intently and gave me the eye contact I desperately longed for as a child who needed validation.

I told her my secrets, like who I had a crush on, and
I also told her about the minutiae of my day. She never
cut me off short or brushed me off. Planting myself on
the floor next to her desk, I kept my eyes on her face.
I wanted to see if she would make any dismissive facial
expressions if and when she determined what I'd said was
crazy or judged that I was *weird*. But she didn't.

She said, "God is trying to rescue you from something." I shared my worries with her, and confided that
I had recurring dreams. Knowing that she was a faith-
based woman who believed in God's redemptive powers,
I felt a weight lifted, as she affirmed my lived experiences.
I no longer asked God to take my life. Instead I thought,
It's not over even if I fail, and when I fall, I won't die. Life as I
knew it presented me with two very clear options: I could
fall, or I could choose to fly.

CHAPTER 12

Thou Shall Not Steal

"I feel like there are women who are genuinely born to be mothers, and women who are born to be aunties, and women who really probably not should be allowed near children. The tragedy that happens is when any one of those women ends up in the wrong category."

~ELIZABETH GILBERT

Katrina and I left unsaid so much of what should be shared or otherwise expressed in a parent-child relationship. I wish I could have expressed my gratitude for those facets of her, which I found to be good despite all of the emotional and physical abuse I was unfairly subjected to. I recognized redeeming qualities in her, I hoped to one day emulate; there were parts I saw as precious which I wanted to love.

I vividly remember when I was eight, nine, and ten wanting so desperately for Katrina to love me. I recall thirsting for her motherly affection as desperately as one might thirst for water after wandering aimlessly in a desert. I needed to be seen, held, and adored by her. I needed Katrina to acknowledge my needs as her child. I remember creating the task of counting all the different reasons to love her.

There was one memorable time I had a serious bout of stomach flu. Earlier in the evening, Katrina had tried a new recipe and baked a tuna casserole with cornflake topping. After eating some, I started to feel queasy and lightheaded, and soon enough I was projectile vomiting from my bedroom all the way to the bathroom. Unusually empathetic for her, she dutifully changed the sheets on my bed and let me sleep in her room that night. It was the first time she allowed me in her room at the new apartment in Little Rock, and it was the first time she had ever allowed me in her bed. That night while I recuperated, she told her girlfriends about me being sick, and she checked on me several times throughout the night. The next day, after placing her hand on my forehead to check for my temperature, she spent the day nursing me back to health with chicken soup and Sprite. I felt like a daughter who was worthy of her love for the first time ever, and I remember wanting to stay sick longer, so I could see more of that compassionate side of her.

During my teenage years, I felt a rare bond with her, as we stood shoulder-to-shoulder at our kitchen table baking pound cake. As the more seasoned baker, she directed me by saying, "Get me the sugar, flour, eggs, and vanilla." Happy to be her assistant, I thought about how I would one day make my own pound cakes, too.

"Before you pour the batter in the Bundt pan, you need to flour it," she said, "Buy real butter. Unsalted brands like Land O'Lakes." Years later and now the head of my own household, I still buy unsalted butter because of her advice.

"Make sure to rub butter on every part of the pan. We don't want any part of the cake to stick." After inspecting my work, she said, "Get that bag of flour and pour some in. Make sure to dust the whole pan, including the sides. Before you're done, tap the pan with the palm of your hand 'til you see the flour has covered the whole surface evenly." Once I finished, she said, "Pour the batter into the Bundt and place it in the oven." She continued, as if she were instructing a classroom.

The steel, circular, cake pan felt as heavy as the cast iron skillet she used to bake cornbread. She directed me on when to turn it so the batter lay evenly. The weight of the pan, along with the responsibility of not dropping it, made my fingers extra vigilant, as I transferred the contents of the Bundt pan into the preheated oven.

I've come to cherish the memories of us cooking together because they were the only times I almost felt somewhat in sync with my biological mother. I can chuckle about it now, but I never quite lost the fear that she might've cut my head off if I didn't do each task perfectly. I can still remember those moments we were standing side-by-side in front of the stove, so close that the hairs on her arm lightly grazed mine. I only wish the memory of those moments were made sweeter, if they'd been a precursor to signs of actual affection. I wished she would have allowed me to nestle my head on her shoulder. I wish she would've planted a kiss on my cheek.

Our cooking lessons together allowed me to see her as a human, a complicated woman, and a mother who had both good and bad days. The cooking lessons helped me to see Katrina as a genuine mother figure—who, in those captive moments while cooking, no matter how brief, demonstrated her capacity to be a parent to me. It was a stark departure from her usual everyday act of being the abuser who made my life miserable.

Katrina was a beautiful woman who knew how to play up her good looks and femininity. Sometimes I worked to commit her best facial features to memory, so I could always remember my mother a certain way in my mind. I also admired the way she walked effortlessly in heels. While I was home alone, I sometimes snuck into her closet to touch the softness of her clothing. She ironed, folded, and hung each item in its designated place. I also admired the neatness and the deliberate way in which she took care of her jewelry. She was a tidy person by nature, and she even made a conscious effort to minimize the smell of her Virginia Slims cigarettes by opening the car window a crack and blowing the billows of exhaled smoke in its direction. She flicked the butt as soon as she finished the last puff.

She always smelled divine and wore just enough perfume so others could appreciate her essence. Bottles of Oscar de la Renta, Issey Miyake, Elizabeth Arden, and Christian Dior were placed neatly on the corners of her dresser. Once or twice, I snuck into her room to spray my neck before school. She had the smoothest skin, and when puberty made its entrance, she took me to the doctor to get an acne prescription. Clear skin mattered so much to her that one night, right after she beat me and left marks along my forearms, thighs, and shins, she turned in my direction and nonchalantly asked, "What are you wearing to school tomorrow? Make sure you wear something to hide the scars." Shocked by how cavalier she sounded, I could only shrug my shoulders in response.

Dealing with the contradiction of mixed feelings that each beating brought, I always had to re-convince myself that she cared about me in the slightest. As I sat on the toilet, after this particular beating, I was still catching my breath. I recall placing my fingers along each fresh bruise, noting its size, and questioning if it would swell or turn from red to purple the next day.

Both strangers and those on Katrina's side of the family—sometimes one in the same—often remarked, "You look just like your Momma, just a darker version." In those moments, I wished I could hide under a rock and shed my likeness of her like a snake would shed its skin.

I didn't like these side-by-side comparisons especially because it made me question the drive behind Katrina's incessant beatings.

Maybe it's because I looked like her, that Katrina also took an interest in the tutelage of my appearance. She often said to me, "When you wear makeup it should look natural. People shouldn't automatically know you're wearing it. Use just enough to highlight your features." Katrina's makeup, more often than not, was flawless.

I loved the way she spent time putting on her eye shadow, applying blush to the apples of her cheeks, and thoughtfully choosing the shade of her lipstick. Before school one morning during my fifth-grade year, I took the opportunity to go into her bathroom and sample for myself every piece of makeup she owned in the effort to replicate her look. I inspected the powders, used her fine brushes, and tried various shades of blush. I put the makeup products on, one by one, adding anything that looked like it might make me pretty. Having lingered too long, I was suddenly rushing to catch the school bus, so I left in a hurry leaving behind trace specks and smudges all over the counter. I thought, *I'll clean it when I get home.*

With a face full of foundation, blush, and merlot lipstick, I did a double take in the mirror. I said to myself, I look older now and pretty. Everybody's gonna compliment me. Having lingered too long, I then returned to my bedroom and retrieved six pairs of white cotton ankle socks from my dresser. Envisioning Dolly Parton's buxom chest, I placed three pair of socks into each side of my white 32A training bra. At night, I often read the National Enquirer and prayed to God for a bosom as voluptuous as Dolly's. I laughed victoriously all the way to the bus stop.

When I got into class, one of the kids looked at me and pointed. "What's that in your shirt?" I hadn't realized the balled-up socks created lumps, bumps, and ridges, resembling crinkled pieces of paper under my T-shirt. Taking the socks out one by one, defeated, I threw them across the floor towards my classmates.

When I arrived home from school, thinking I'd gotten away with my act of mischief, I headed straight to the bathroom to wash off the makeup. Unfortunately, I hadn't considered the possibility that my mother would arrive home before I did.

Upon seeing me, she immediately lost her temper and yelled, "You sneaky little bitch. We aren't the same complexion. Your dumb ass wasted all my damn makeup all over the counter."

* * *

Still, when I turned thirteen, she took me to the mall and bought me my first eyeliner, mascara, and lipstick. It was my first coming of age memory. She took me to Victoria's Secret and purchased the designer bras and fancy underwear because she believed looks matter. She also advised me to always wear nice underwear and bras in the event of emergencies where I'd be stripped down to my bare essentials in an ambulance. I imagined myself as a sophisticated adult buying my own matching black lace panty and bra sets. I loved floral patterns and pictured myself as an urbane adult, walking out of the store holding a pink pinstripe Victoria's Secret bag filled with perfectly folded, lacy, flower-embroidered panties. Katrina didn't just inspire visions of being fashion-forward, she unintentionally helped me to envision my future self as an adult who could one day be beautiful, independent, and strong. Her lack of positive encouragement forced me to uplift myself. She helped me to realize that there would come a day when I wouldn't be her punching bag. One day, I would rise above expectation and become the person she didn't yet see in me—trustworthy, beautiful, loved, and successful. There would come a day when my scars and my story would no longer be hidden. She would no longer be allowed to call herself my *mother*—a title she never earned.

Although I know there are no specific physical features of abusers, as a child I felt she operated in kind of an undercover manner. Katrina existed in the world with survival skills akin to those of a chameleon; she learned how to hide, change, and react depending on her given environment. I admired her sense of fashion. She often wore designer apparel, name brands found in expensive boutiques or stores such as Dillard's. With fifty-two weeks in a year, she rarely repeated an outfit when seen in public, especially at church. Her closets were filled with suits and dresses, sometimes so new the tags were still hanging. Shoeboxes and hanging shoe racks were filled. I often wondered how she could afford suits costing $150-$200 each. When we attended church or visited her friends, she always received compliments. As a love-starved kid, I remember thinking I wanted to be admired by people, too.

CHAPTER 13

The Bad

By the time I was twelve or thirteen, most kids I knew my age were beginning to choose their own clothes and had a personal style. I wanted so badly to fit in with my peers, but I never had any input on our shopping choices. Three pairs of pants, four shirts, and one pair of Nikes were spread neatly on my bed, preselected for me. Katrina said, "Try these on, and see if they fit. Do you like them?" School started the following Monday, so I stuffed my complaints and took what I could get. But I wondered, *Why can't I pick out my own stuff?*

Sometime later, Katrina grabbed her keys off the rack and said, "Come on. Let's go to the mall." I got excited because we were going to the extravagant one with four floors on the better side of town. When we arrived at

University Mall, she grabbed her camel-brown hobo bag from the back seat. As we entered the Express store, she said, "Keep an eye out for the clerk. White bitches always watching me."

I watched as she took two of each item off the rack. With clothing hanging from her fingers and draped across her arm, she raised her hand to get the clerk's attention and asked for a dressing room. Walking behind the clerk, she split the shirts, dresses, and slacks into two stacks, giving me six or seven items to hold. After the clerk unlocked the dressing rooms, Katrina motioned for me to join her in the same room. She rolled some items neatly into an oversized shopping bag; she changed the prices on others by switching a clearance tag with a regular price tag. At the cash register, she paid about $50 when the stolen goods were worth three or four times as much. Once we reached the car, she hid the items in her trunk underneath blankets and other clothing.

"This stays here until Darryl goes to work," she said.

The comment bemused me; didn't Darryl know her? As a child, I didn't understand her need to keep stealing a secret from him, considering she'd done much worse— especially to me. What she didn't keep she sold to family and friends, some of whom belonged to our church. After the first time I acted as her accomplice, she often directed me to serve as her lookout. On one occasion, she said, "Let's go. I need to go to Dillard's. I need a new comforter." She selected a cream-colored, king-size, comforter set and headed towards the register.

As she walked, her pace quickened and she said, "Hurry up! They can't catch you once you reach the parking lot." In the background, I could hear the clerk saying, "Stop! You can't take that! Somebody call security!" We ran through Dillard's with the comforter set in hand; I could hear the security officers chasing us from behind. The security guards stopped once they reached the door.

One of the last times I assisted her in stealing, we went back to Express—again armed with a large shopping bag. While walking from the front of the store to the back, she grabbed several items and dropped them in the bag. Standing between the racks, I watched as she stole hundreds of dollars' worth of merchandise.

One of the clerks, a white female who looked to be in her twenties, caught her stealing and said, "Ma'am, I need you to open your bag."

Scared, I stood there thinking, *What if we go to jail?*

Katrina said, "I haven't done anything. I don't have to let you search my bags."

The clerk replied, "I saw you take those blouses off the rack and stuff them in your bag. If you don't let me search, I will call the cops."

Katrina indignantly replied, "Call them."

I didn't have anything in my hand, but I felt sick in the pit of my stomach for being with her. Then Katrina pulled my arm. "Run!"

We once again ran through the mall with security chasing us all the way to the parking garage. As we ran, putting distance between us and the guards, I couldn't shake the thought, I should *just stop now and* tell the officers where we live and about all the other times she's stolen. I wanted her arrested.

* * *

Sundays were a day to dress up in stolen goods, perform, and get praise for the show we put on. We attended Mount Glory Missionary Baptist Church in Jacksonville, Arkansas, a traditional African-American church. Katrina and many other women came dressed in colorful suits, oversized hats, and heels. Our seat assignment stayed the same—left corner of the third-row pew. The service began after two deacons, who stood behind the communion table, led the congregation in singing a hymn. The mothers of the church, sitting in the front left of the sanctuary, joined in. At the next verse, Katrina would chime in, taking over the song by singing louder than anyone else in the church. Then the preaching began, and she "amen-ed" and waved her hands all through the service.

The organ player often backed up the preacher's sermons with up-tempo music, a method of playing that emphasized the sermon's climax and prepared the congregation for a breakout of shouting and dancing. As the pastor shuffled his feet to the music and paced from one end of the pulpit to the other, my mother's dramatic performance would begin. With flailing limbs, she'd jump, dance, fall backwards, and eventually pass out. The

ushers rushed to fan her and cover her with a white bed
sheet. Sometimes she'd fall on the floor in between the
pews. It took three to four ushers to keep her from hurting
herself or others when she jumped and danced as if she
had been overtaken by an *unholy* ghost.

Each Sunday after the service had ended, and we'd
buckled our seatbelts, she'd say, "So how'd I do? Tell me,
how did I look?" Then she'd take the first drag of her cigarette, as I gave her an accounting of how others reacted
to her performance.

For a year or two when we first moved to Little Rock,
she worked as the church secretary. I watched married
men fawn over her, as we passed them during the offering, and the same men would later visit her at home. Men
twice her age were drawn to her. After hearing muffled
noises in her bedroom one day, I tiptoed to her door and
caught a glimpse of the head deacon, a married man in
his 70s, grinding against her naked frame with a blanket
half-covering his body. On another occasion, while we
were in the church office making the weekly bulletin, she
asked me to step out, as he walked in. As I passed him, he
planted a kiss on Katrina's cheek.

She'd brag openly about men paying her for sex.
Once, she brazenly took me on a date between her and
a married man to watch the movie *Rosewood*. During the
car ride home, after the date, she talked about the money
he gave her and how she liked having sex with him. She
made me a witness to parts of her life I didn't want to
see. Ultimately, her experiences and her dealings with the

opposite sex made me more wary of men. It reinforced a formative belief that stayed with me for years to come: men will hurt, cheat, abuse, and leave. I guess she forgot or gave little consideration to the fact that I was just a child.

CHAPTER 14

Out of Body

God, if someone abducted me or mistakenly placed me in the arms of this woman, please let my *real parents* find me. While looking at my reflection in the mirror after another painful encounter with Katrina, I couldn't accept the version of my bleak day-to-day life in which I belonged to Katrina, and she belonged to me. Lord, if her real child was out there, I hope they're loved and free of abuse. I refused to accept Katrina was the mother God planned for me.

I was around ten years old at the time, and before I said this prayer, I had accidentally broken her porcelain duck salt shaker. Somehow the salt shaker had fallen from the counter and broken into several pieces. I threw away the broken pieces without another thought. Moments later, however, when Katrina asked about the duck's whereabouts, I shrugged my shoulders, lied, and said I didn't know. We stood in the kitchen, both glancing at the single porcelain pepper shaker sitting on the window ledge. She raised her hand and slapped me, the force of which made my head spin in the opposite direction. Then she immediately retreated to get her leather belt, leaving me in the kitchen to think about my dishonesty. She returned with a vengeance wildly swinging the belt, whipping me, pushing, and shoving me, while I endured lash after lash.

"You ...will ...not ...lie. You ...are ...gonna ...quit ... being ...a ...fucking ...liar." Over and over, she continued yelling and cursing at me, as if she wanted the whole neighborhood to hear. Even if they heard her words or my cries, I knew deep down by this point that no one would come to my aid. She continued the whipping until her breath became labored, and she'd broken out into a sweat. It terrified me to think of what she might be capable of, as her beatings became increasingly more brutal over the years. While hitting me, she waited for a response. "Oh, you're not gonna cry?" She hit me more forcefully with each lash along my back, head, face, legs, buttocks, arms, and chest. She seemed to find satisfaction in my pleading and screaming. I wailed in anguish and begged for her to stop; I was wheezing so much I thought I might stop breathing. Satiated, she finally stopped and wiped the sweat from her brow, as she turned and walked away into her bedroom.

Afterwards, I stood naked in front of the bathroom mirror counting each bruise: "One, two, three, four ..." I took an inventory of the damage incurred by each body part. Sitting on the cold porcelain toilet provided me with some relief while I waited for the bathtub to fill with warm water. Looking at each bruise, some red, others purple, some with broken skin and others raised and swollen, I thought as I always did when things went too far, *I wonder if I can hide them under my clothing?* After the bath, I chose jeans and a long shirt to wear to school the next day.

* * *

Some kids grow up getting spanked, but knew their parents loved them even when there was corporal punishment. For me, I believed the opposite. When Katrina hit me, I believed she was expressing exactly how she felt about me. Maybe this was all there was.

Not only was I the usual victim of Katrina's physical violence, I was also a constant target of her emotional abuse which contributed to an ongoing and increasing sense of anxiety about everyone and everything I encountered in my young life. I remember the day Katrina and I went to the pediatrician's office for my annual physical, when I was eight or nine years old and getting ready for fourth grade. The nurse called my name and led me to the exam room. She wore latex gloves and held a small towelette and a specimen jar with a white top. She said, "Sweetie, use the towelette to clean from front to back."

Holding the plastic cup between her thumb and index finger, she said, "Afterwards, urinate into the cup as much
as you can. When you get to the top of the cup, continue
urinating in the toilet. Put the top back on and wipe off
any urine." I nodded, knowing I didn't understand the
instructions. Crouching in front of the toilet with the cup
between my shaky little hands, I began to pee in the cup,
but the pee came out fast and sprayed everywhere.

Forgetting the nurse's directions, I kept peeing even
as the cup overflowed, making a mess of everything.
Afterwards, I looked in disbelief at the royal mess I had
on my hands. I began cleaning myself and made things
worse by using toilet paper to wipe the floor. I hesitated
to leave the room, unsure of what to say about my urine-
soaked pants. When the nurse knocked on the door to
check on me, I said, "I accidentally peed on myself." The
nurse said with compassion, "That's OKAY. You aren't
the first. Let me get your mom to help clean you up."

When Katrina opened the door and took stock of
what happened, she was far less understanding and said,
"You fucking dumbass. How'd you pee on yourself?"
Without a thought for my feelings, she embarrassed me
in front of the kind nurse, who was standing by. Looking
at the nurse, whose lips were now pursed, Katrina put
on a fake smile, and said, "I guess we can call her Miss
*Pee*body." As we were leaving, Katrina baited me again,
"How does it feel to be Miss Peebody?" When we got
home, she looked at Anthony and said, "Guess who has
a new nickname? That's Miss *Peebody* right there. She's

too stupid to know how to pee in a cup." Katrina called her friends and repeated the story for the next few weeks, laughing at my expense.

Countless diminishing experiences like this one were par for the course during my life with Katrina, and the simplest of tasks began to befuddle me. Because my self-esteem was so battered, and because my stress response was always in high gear, I often lost the ability to hear or respond to others constructively. This mental blank slate happened even when I was addressed by a neutral third-party adult, like the well-meaning and kind nurse. There were so many things I felt I had to bottle up inside, because I didn't yet know how to express myself or ask for help.

CHAPTER 15

Banana Bread

By the time puberty hit, I was far different from the happy-go-lucky child I'd once been. In her place, was a pre-teen who was awkward, out-of-sorts, and paranoid. In class, I ranged from performing at an average level to well below average in science and math. No matter how early I went to bed, I was chronically restless for most of the night and slept no more than three or four hours nightly. And then, arriving at school, and within minutes of getting settled at my desk, I'd promptly fall asleep. My brain felt inundated by the constant assault of new information and junior high expectations.

Sitting in a room full of people, overwhelmed my senses so much that I blocked everything out and tried to mentally enter a quiet place. Walking in the halls with hundreds of other people caused me social anxiety, as I didn't feel comfortable with unexpected touches or anyone walking too closely behind me. The sound of the bell, the squeak of a door, or an unexpected "hello" caused me to jump. I was oblivious to what was going on with anyone outside of myself. When I wasn't having anxiety dreams about forgetting my locker combination, I was actually forgetting my locker combination. Countless visits to the guidance counselor's office to retrieve the code became embarrassing. I used my locker several times a day every single day, yet even after six months, there were occasions when I was under so much stress that I still forgot the combination. There were also times when I stood in the halls between classes with a vacant mind, forgetting which class to attend next. On those days, I found myself back in the guidance counselor's office asking for a copy of my schedule.

I surveyed the cafeteria at lunch, looking for someone who was sitting alone and wouldn't mind company. I hated free time outside of class because it made me acutely aware of my loneliness. Unlike some kids, I didn't have a core group of friends to spend recess and lunch with. I also spent a lot of idle time feeling envious about privileges I perceived other kids had, while I was always going without. Some kids brought lunch from home, and I automatically saw them as being more loved than I was because someone had taken the time to shop for the food, prepare the food, and pack the food. Someone cared enough to remind those kids to place their lunches in their backpacks each morning. Sometimes, I witnessed parents bringing forgotten lunches to the school office. In all my years growing up under Katrina's roof, I never once learned what it felt like to own a lunch box and drink from a thermos or juice box.

I remember the girl who brought homemade banana bread to school. She had hazel eyes and long, stringy, blonde hair held in place with a barrette on both sides. We sat at the same lunch table, she with her *Strawberry Shortcake* lunchbox, and me with a tan, plastic, school lunch tray that held a Styrofoam plate containing a sloppy joe, corn, peaches, and chocolate milk. When I asked her about the bread, she said, "My grandma made it for me last night. It's rotten banana bread. She bit the corner of the bread first. She looked at it, taking a few bites, and then examined the small piece she held between her fingers.

My mouth salivated, as I watched. How could anyone make something so delicious out of rotten bananas? Years later, as an adult, I would recall this memory and make banana bread for myself, too, but without any emotional satisfaction. I imagined her grandma as a loving member of their household. Someone who found a new purpose for everything, including overripened bananas. I visualized her standing in a sunlit kitchen, lovingly preparing the bread for her granddaughter. I remember her and my other classmates regularly opening little notes that said, "I love you" or "Have a good day" or "I'm proud of you." My emotional needs were so unmet, I had to fight the strong urge to scour through the trash and keep the Post-it Notes for myself.

One day as I passed through the hallway, I noticed a group of my classmates huddled in the corner beside their lockers. I overheard one of the popular girls bragging about her parents redecorating her room for her birthday—they had painted her room in her favorite shade of purple. I imagined my classmate looking at paint swatches and selecting her favorite color. She talked about how they had updated her room with new furniture and a matching purple and white comforter set. I imagined her parents going to Target to pick out wall décor, lamps, and rugs. I wanted a room like hers so much, I convinced myself that purple was my favorite color.

I wished my room contained items I liked. Instead, after Anthony graduated from high school, and after he joined the Navy, Katrina transferred my belongings into his room. There was no change of furniture or décor. Besides my clothes, music, and books, nothing in the room belonged to me or represented my tastes. The four-poster, cherrywood, queen bedroom set in my room had first belonged to Katrina, was passed down to Anthony, and was later made available for my secondhand use. I couldn't help but wonder how many immoralities were committed in that bed. For the first few nights, I stayed awake agonizing over being in that room; I wholeheartedly believed each piece of furniture held un indescribable evil spirit. *Why couldn't I have my own space, my own body, and make my own choices about where I wanted to live and sleep?* Almost nothing in my life was actually mine.

CHAPTER 16

Inspiration

"Through it all, still I survive."

~ME

Halfway through the school year, I became the target of about four or five girls from the McAlmott neighborhood in North Little Rock, a part of town where the Bloods, Crips, crack cocaine addicts, poor folks, and church folk all resided. It was the kind of neighborhood where people who weren't used to such areas locked their car doors as they drove down the street. A girl named Brandy had singled me out and said, "You act like you all that, walking the halls acting stuck up." I turned my head and took a step back, unsure of whether she was talking to me. As she and her friend began to encroach on my personal space, she said, "You walking around like you too good to talk to people, looking like a nerd." She looked at her friend and said, "You know, she's probably one of them girls that make the honor roll." With few friends, I didn't have a posse of allies who could protect me. Brandy and her friends teased and taunted me beginning in seventh grade. The bullying continued until I graduated from high school.

Brandy didn't know me or know that I thought about death daily. The girls spread rumors about plans to jump me. On the days when they needed someone to pick on, I feared they would catch me off guard, and I wouldn't be able to protect myself. I feared being embarrassed in front of hordes of children if they were to get the better of me, by kicking and punching me. Brandy and her friends had no reservations about stealing my purse. She also broke the zipper of my red San Francisco 49ers Starter jacket. One day, they chased me down the hall, until I reached the principal's office where I told the first adult I encountered about the girls chasing me and taking my items. The girls seeing me tattle-tale, as we used to call it, returned back to class and did not bother me for a few weeks after that incident.

After school, I entered a mental tunnel to help me cope with the stress at home. I felt sometimes robotic, without feeling, as if I were going through the motions of day-to-day responsibilities. My life after school included coming home to phone calls or notes directing me to look

in the sink and, if there was meat thawing, to cook it. I
prepared a lot of fried chicken and pork chops, collard
greens, Jiffy cornbread, and white rice. On one occasion,
Katrina came into the kitchen to check on my progress.
Picking up the spoon and dipping it into the cast iron
skillet, she tasted my brown, chunky, smothered chicken
gravy. Slamming the spoon down on the stove, she said,
"Why'd you cut the onions so goddamn big?" Shaking
her head, she stared straight at me and yelled, "We can't
eat this!" Her caustic words were always demeaning me.
When she stomped out of the kitchen she said, "You'll
never be anything 'cause you don't know how to fucking
cook. When you grow up, no man is going to want you.
You'll probably end up getting your ass beat." I recall this
"cooking lesson" so vividly that I can tell you my exact
age—twelve—what I was wearing, and the month when
it occurred. Some things are impossible to forget.

* * *

Part of my daily ritual as a pre-teen was to call my
cousin Lynn, who was Maurice's brother's daughter. She
and I were pre-teens and lived within thirty minutes of
each other in Little Rock. When I was home alone, I'd
often tell her everything that transpired with Katrina.
It was a great outlet to have someone to confide in and
growing up, we were closer than white on rice. As I cried
and vented about each incident of abuse, Lynn found a
way to bring me comfort and laughter.

During one of our after-school phone conversations, I laughed and said, "This lady is crazy. I think she has a mental block." We both giggled, having no idea what the words actually meant, but also knowing what we were trying to convey to each other by using the words.

A few days later, Katrina called from work and said, "Get ready. We need to go to the mall." Thinking nothing of the call and hearing nothing unusual in the flatness of her voice, I met her outside, as she pulled into the driveway. On the way, she took long drags from her cigarette and listened to the radio; it was a silent ride as usual.

Entering the mall parking lot, she stopped the car abruptly and said, "You didn't know, but I'm recording you and Lynn's conversations. I've been listening to everything y'all say. I know everything. You talk a lot of shit about me."

I tried to remember anything and everything I'd said. Still sitting in the lane between rows of parking spaces, she raised her hand and slapped the left side of my face, knocking my head towards the window.

She said, "So, you don't like the bass in my speakers, and you think I have a *mental block?*" Looking away from her, I held my hand against my cheek and couldn't help but smile, as I heard her repeating my words.

Following this incident, my phone calls to Lynn were prohibited. Since I could no longer call Lynn to share my secrets, I began writing in diaries and journals. Writing my thoughts and creating poetry allowed my mind to heal as my words filled the pages. I wrote about how much I hated my mother. I wrote about my interior landscape.

When she rummaged through my room and found my diary one day, she said, "So, you hate me, huh?" I wanted to say, "Well, yes, Mother Dear, I do, and it's about time you know it." But I stood motionless, waiting for my punishment. She took away my diary and shared its contents with family and friends in an effort to shame me, but I continued writing in my school binders and notebooks.

My inspiration for writing came from having no other emotional outlet. I used to sit in my room and write until the sides of my fingers became too red and tender to hold the pencil. Reading and writing helped me to escape the real world. It opened my eyes to an imagined future I might be able to embrace one day, and it allowed me to dream.

One of my earliest female role models was Aunt Faye, who was one of Momma's daughters. She introduced me to poetry and black authors. At the time, she lived down the street from Momma, and I was only twelve years old. Aunt Faye was one of the most talented members of the family. She was the creative entrepreneur type, and I admired her natural style and beauty. Lynn and I would visit her each time we went to Momma's house.

Like Aunt Yolanda, Aunt Faye made us laugh and made us temporarily forget our problems. She filled the role of a self-defining black feminist before I knew such a title existed. On visits to Momma's house, she handed me books and said, "Here, you need to read this. Always read and get your education. That's something no one can take from you."

Because of her, I read books by Nikki Giovanni, Langston Hughes, Gwendolyn Brooks, and Maya Angelou. I looked up to Maya Angelou not just because of her poetry but also because she, too, survived childhood sexual abuse. She, too, suffered the fallout and post-traumatic stress of her abuse for years after the incident. The authors I read spoke for me in ways I didn't yet have the capacity to assert or advocate for myself. When I read Maya Angelou's poem, *Phenomenal Woman*, I read it in silence and then aloud. I followed each line with my fingers, curious as to whether I could rise to one day calling myself "phenomenal."

Reading the works of brown and black authors encouraged me and gave me strength. They wrote about being black in America and surviving struggle, and they gave me insight into my identity that taught me more than I would ever learn in school. During my childhood, *Chicken Soup for the Soul* books were best sellers. I avidly consumed the series, and I lost myself in the stories of people who had lost, healed, and survived. The one item Katrina allowed me to own was my books; she'd even buy me some every now and then. Others were gifted by my family in Pine Bluff or borrowed from the library. I dreamed of one day telling my own story, one with a happy ending. When my dream of love and happiness finally came true, in a time not so far in the distant past,

I once again took pencil to paper to write down the story you are reading today.

Reading and writing poetry helped me to feel in control. The act of reading and writing grounded me, and by doing so, allowed my thoughts to roam free. It was the one place where I could be honest. I imagined publishing my own works, just like the poets I looked up to. For reasons I don't yet understand, inspiration always arrives on the heels of great stress. Poetry became the salve I needed to tolerate my pain, which on some days felt like an unbearable burden. One of my most memorable poems was inspired by my love of Maya Angelou's "Still I Rise." The words I authored for myself read:

> *Life hasn't always been so nice.*
> *It's given me heartache, pains, sorrowful times*
> *Thunder and rain ...*
> *But through it all still I survive.*
> *Through it all still I survive ...*

CHAPTER 17

Influencer

Some people have one mother; others have three or four when counting biological mothers, stepmothers, and mothers-in-law. As for me, Oprah is the one: mother, mentor, and muse. Her influence on me has not only been enormous, but life-saving.

No, seriously. I'm the daughter Oprah gave birth to from afar, so to speak. It was around the age of fourteen when I first remember paying close attention to her, while working in Katrina's storefront beauty shop. I'd just finished shampooing a woman's Jheri-curled hair, when Katrina turned on *The Oprah Winfrey Show*. After washing my hands, I walked towards the television, which sat in the corner of the shop nearest the door. I wouldn't have ordinarily paid much attention except that Katrina said, "Oprah don't do nothing for black people. She sho' keeps some white women on her show. Look at her audience, nothing but white people ..."

My ears perked up, as I zeroed in on the audience, one with a majority of white women wearing bold-colored sweaters with shoulder pads. I can't remember what they were talking about, but I remember feeling a familial kinship with Oprah right away. I believed anyone Katrina spoke ill of, must be a person worth my attention and hopefully my adoration. From that day forward, I found myself immersed in the *Oprah show*, paying little attention to the guests but more so to Oprah's direct, conversational interview style. I wanted to know why she resonated with people all across the world. I wanted to know her secret on how to build bridges with people who didn't look like us. I wanted to know her story, and if we had anything in common.

After years of watching the show and listening to her interviews, I realized we have a few similarities. For instance, Oprah lived with her grandmother for the first six years of her life, and then reunited with her mother. The courts removed me from my grandmother's home at the same age. Both of our grandmothers introduced us to God. Oprah's mom attempted to take her to a group home; Katrina threatened to drop me off on several occasions. Yet I never lived in one, and neither did Oprah. We both love Dr. Maya Angelou, too; I grew up reading *I Know Why Caged Bird Sings*. Oprah read Dr. Angelou's autobiography and has stated many times the deep impact it had on her life; similarly, I began writing poetry because

Dr. Angelou gave me the courage to. Additionally, Oprah and I were both sexually abused. She didn't tell anyone until she became an adult, and I did the same. Like Oprah, I loved *The Color Purple*—not the book (I've never read it), but the movie. I've watched that movie more times than I can count. Furthermore, Oprah has a book club—and I have books, lots and lots of books, too. I grew up reading because it was the only activity I could engage in without getting in trouble. Each poet I read gave me insight and helped me to discern for myself what it meant to be a black woman, an overcomer, and a survivor who has surmounted her biggest obstacles and lived to tell about it. Oprah's skin is as black as mine, her lips are as full as mine, and her figure is curvy like mine. Oprah, to me, embodies a holy trinity of motherhood, mentorship, and inspiration. If she can use her pain to inspire and galvanize hearts and minds, why can't I?

CHAPTER 18

Sparing the Rod

Sometimes I allow myself to believe my mother simply wanted to teach me everything she wished someone had taught her but hadn't. Perhaps she wanted me to learn to be an honest, respectful, self-sufficient woman who didn't have to cheat, steal, hustle, or compromise to survive. Maybe she loved me in the only language she understood—violence.

My mother was born in June 1960 and grew up in the South during a time when people believed spanking was the surest way to discipline a child. They believed in using corporal punishment to correct children, and thought nothing else of it. Call it overly hopeful, but I believe that had she been taught a different way to parent, and a better way to discipline, she would have.

I have often wondered if my thoughts surrounding my childhood are overly dramatic—perhaps my own bias keeps me from seeing Katrina as she truly is. Various times throughout my life, I've rationalized my experiences as being the norm. I blamed myself for being too awkward, emotional, overly sensitive, and taking people and things too seriously at times. I faulted myself for the times I lied about things that made no sense for normal, well-adjusted kids to lie about. Perhaps, I have a blind side, and I'm only able to see and defend my own truth. My truth is that the beatings and much of my upbringing was abusive.

I'll admit that much, though we don't have to look far to see debates regarding the psycho-social effects of corporal punishment on young people. I grew up in a school that still allowed principals and teachers to spank children—and I have first-hand experience receiving some of those spankings. Once, when I wouldn't shut my mouth in fourth grade, my homeroom teacher, Ms. Quick, walked with me down to the principal's office. At first, I wasn't sure what to expect, as I glanced from wall to wall, taking in filing cabinets that were overly full with student records, mounds of papers piled up high on the principal's desk, and college degrees framed and hanging on the wall directly behind him.

In an exasperated tone, my teacher justified herself saying, "I just can't get her to sit down. I've told her five or six times to quiet down, but she's bent on doing the opposite. I can't even get through my lesson before she's out of her seat again." Afterwards, she returned to the classroom, leaving me to stand there questioning my fate.

Principal Bennett stood up from his desk and demanded that I bend over, grab the sides of the desk, and keep my head facing forward. As I looked at the wall, I noticed Mr. Bennett grab the heavy, wooden paddle. He reminded me to keep my hands out of the way and then swiftly - smack, smack, smack - he hit me with the paddle board so hard that my butt continued to sting when I returned to my desk to sit down. The stinging, burning sensation left me with the same sense of injustice and helplessness felt after one of Katrina's thrashings. Even in school, I couldn't escape.

The use of that form of discipline reinforced for me that abuse can and will happen anywhere. My body was not safe at home or at school. Children are taught to tell a trusted adult when someone hurts them—but who could I tell when home and school alike were places of danger? Corporal punishment, and the outright uncontrolled rages I'd been on the receiving end of for years, not only marked by body physically, but also battered my self-esteem into such an advanced state of deterioration that my trauma symptoms persisted throughout my adult years. The secrecy I bound myself to about the ongoing abuse at home led me to feel shame and defenseless vulnerability for years to come. Today, most states have outlawed the use of corporal punishment in schools and have replaced it with in-school suspension, behavior plans, positive reinforcement, and collaboration with guidance counselors and school social workers to help a child thrive. If I'd been a recipient of such proactive aid during my school years, perhaps, I would have felt *seen* and been treated for my debilitating pain. Instead, in order to fit in and detract any more unwanted attention from myself, which often proved to result in corporal punishment, I made myself small. I made myself meek, and as a result, was ignored by those living in closest proximity to me.

CHAPTER 19

Shhhh...

When I was beaten at home, Darryl, far from ever being an engaged father figure, remained out of sight, like an ostrich putting his head in the sand. One time, when I was in my room consoling myself after putting up with another merciless beating by Katrina, Darryl came to check on me and timidly stated in a boyish, surrendering tone, "I can't get involved because if I do, she gets mad at me." He spoke to me in a quiet voice, the way two employees might talk to each other in their cubicles when they don't want the boss to hear.

The only time we had these discussions was when he knew Katrina had stepped out of the house or had to work late. Whenever we were all home at the same time, he avoided me as if a simple acknowledgment of my presence was too much. One afternoon, when I'd just arrived home from school with books still in hand, he approached me. Holding the doorknob and standing with his head peeking out of his partially closed bedroom door, he said, "When I try to say something, she yells, curses, and calls me names. Believe me, I've tried, but she won't talk to me. She withholds sex for at least a week if I even mention your name." At sixteen, as I stood in the hallway, listening to the henpecked admission, I felt I had more power in my pinkie toe than he had as a fully-grown man in his mid-forties.

He stated, "I feel bad for you. I don't know why she treats you that way. Something is wrong with her. I try to talk to her, but she doesn't listen."

I headed to my room, shaking my head in disbelief. I also remember feeling somewhat sorry for him. Katrina was a deeply flawed person, and I questioned why he chose to stay with her. Maybe he understood her in a way no one else could? It sometimes felt as if he and I were in the same boat. I couldn't pretend I didn't know who really wore the pants in the house, so none of what he said to me came as a surprise. His admission validated for me that no one, including the only other adult in the home, would come to my rescue. Bravery was a rare quality that I was unacquainted with until later in life when I met strong and mature individuals who would choose to stand by my side.

CHAPTER 20

My Other Half

I heard God whisper, "You don't need an example; all you need is me…"

~ME

After Maurice moved to Colorado, I visited him and his family on three occasions between the ages of six and seventeen. All three times, I felt like an unwelcome guest, and was treated as such. Three times, the superficiality of our interactions or the fearful place from which we both operated forced me to reassess my thoughts about the man who I'd hoped would be a true father to me but wasn't. I had placed him on such a high pedestal over the years, that it was a truly painful awakening to come to terms with the hard truth that he didn't *want* to father me. When I had especially turbulent times with Katrina, which were often, I would find emotional refuge in creating an image for myself of a daddy who loved me for who I was and protected me at all costs. When Katrina proved to be untrustworthy of my love and adoration with each violent transgression, I would funnel all my hopes and dreams for a loving relationship with a parent through daydreams about Maurice. Settled in Colorado, he had his own family and a daughter, not me, who was the apple of his eye. I was a reminder of a life he'd already left behind.

In his physical absence, Maurice made an effort to send cards and money for my birthday and important holidays, which I cherished receiving. During our guarded telephone conversations, I withheld my excitement, as he started with the most generic of questions, "How's school?" As I didn't get to see him or touch his face, I hung on to every word. As soon as one phone call concluded, I couldn't wait to hear from him again. I dreamed about a reunion in which he would lift me off of my feet and give me a bear hug. I'd lose myself in daydreams about how much I loved him, and filled in a narrative I needed to tell myself about how much he loved me. I imagined time spent in conversation with him which I wished would come to fruition one day. I looked up to the man who had left Arkansas for better opportunities and was working multiple jobs to provide for his family. There was a time in my life when the image I upheld of him was so revered that in my mind he could do no wrong.

I unfairly held Katrina responsible for the wedge that existed in my relationship with Maurice, such as when he didn't send for me during the most tumultuous periods of my life. It was only years later, as a working adult, when I found the courage to call him one final time out of the depths of my agonizing loneliness and sorrow. I then discovered the lack of intimacy perceived between us was a choice he had actively made. I always found it difficult to get a sense of Maurice's love for me through random phone calls and Christmas gifts of winter sweaters and leggings (gifts Katrina returned the day after they arrived). Still, a small part of me felt special and remembered, which gave me just enough fortitude and vision to fan the flames of looking forward to seeing him at some undisclosed date in the future.

I daydreamed and ruminated about how my life would have been different if he had been part of it. He was, in my youth, the parent I wanted but couldn't have. I created a complete, perfect version of my father based on what I observed of fatherhood from sitcom TV fathers, or fictionalized fathers I'd read about in books. I created a fantasy of him and, as a substitution for the real thing, lived with him in this hazy fantasy realm. My family, who routinely made a habit of withholding information and being less than candid with me about those I desired to be closer to such as Maurice, remained resoundingly silent when I asked why Maurice didn't visit me, and why I didn't get to talk to him more than once or twice a year.

They said, a bit evasively, "He called last week. He's doing well. I don't know why he hasn't called you." Momma's family said that he always sent flowers, cards, and money on their birthdays. As a child, this confounded me. He remembered them, kept in touch with them, but forgot about me. He preoccupied my day-to-day thoughts so much, that I made a point of asking Momma about him in every conversation I had with her. Achingly, I wanted to hear from him, too.

Sometime after my thirteenth birthday, Katrina stood in the doorway of my bedroom holding a piece of paper and saying the words that would change my outlook forever. "I asked Maurice to start paying child support. He said he wouldn't do anything until we took a DNA test."

I don't recall giving samples of my saliva or blood, but the results of the paternity test further rocked the foundation of my already fragile world. Additionally, up until the day of the test, Katrina had never said anything about the possibility of someone else being my father. Not only that, but she had never mentioned a word about needing money from him. This was a woman who cruelly returned the birthday and Christmas presents Maurice meant for me, and took the money she redeemed for her own personal use. I guilelessly wondered, *How could he not be my father, when I have his last name?*

As she stood between my bedroom doorway and the hallway, still holding the piece of paper close to her face, she said, "Well, the DNA results came back. He is not your father, and I don't know who is." She shrugged her shoulders, nonchalantly. "It might be a guy named Richard, but I don't know. Something fishy is going on. Maurice probably sent his brother to take the test for him."

When she said those words, I tried to decipher the results for myself and consider all of its many implications. I looked at her closely, trying to detect any sign of empathy, tenderness, or the slightest consideration for how this news would affect me. She wouldn't look me in the eye. The way she shrugged her shoulders and walked away, was the most cavalier and hurtful thing I'd ever witnessed. After that day, she never brought the subject up again. But she felt no qualms about further separating me from my allegiance to Momma by telling me Momma *wasn't* my grandma. The aunts, uncles, and cousins I'd grown up with and known as the only surrogate family I'd had in the absence of Katrina and Maurice during my earliest years weren't related to me. The only family I'd ever considered to be my family *wasn't*. I didn't have a real, living parent in my life outside of her. My daydreams about being Maurice's cherished daddy's girl came crashing down around me. She said half of my biology was unknown, and when she said it, she couldn't look me in the eye. She couldn't hug me in consolation for my loss, and she did not offer any apology.

At the time, I'd often speculated about whose physical features I most resembled. I also wanted the security of knowing I belonged to someone in this world. I needed to know that the parts of me I couldn't explain—like my personality, my interests, and my idiosyncrasies—mirrored those of someone who shared my DNA. It hurt me beyond words knowing that my genetic makeup was anyone's guess. It hurt me even more realizing it was very possible that some guy was out there—my real father—going through life unaware I even existed. Having a biological connection to those I loved felt even more important because, unlike someone who is adopted—and chosen—my parents had depreciated my sense of self-worth by their acts of leaving me, dropping me off, and choosing someone better to nurture and love.

Time stopped as I fought back tears. I cringed at the thought of Katrina's promiscuity. Maybe at the time I was conceived, Katrina had been with many, many men. Wild presumptions began to run amok in my head. Maybe Maurice cared more about saving money than being there for his child—maybe he did give his ID to his brother. Maybe Katrina knew the truth and had lied to him and everyone else for thirteen years. Maybe she knew the truth and didn't want the real father to know. Again, knowing Katrina's penchant for manipulation, anything seemed possible.

After telling Momma and my extended family, I'd hoped they'd offer a bit of solace for the emptiness and rage I held within. Much to my crushing disappointment, they reacted to the news first with silence, then with blank stares and less than comforting excuses.

"I don't know why Katrina would say that. He never said he wasn't your father."

And, "She's only trying to hurt you. That man is your daddy. You look like him."

But did I? I needed them to share in my shock, anger, and frustration.

After another long pause, Momma remarked, "You're still my daughter, no matter what. Even though you're my granddaughter, I love you like you're my own. I always have and always will."

At the time, I felt like no one except me understood the gravity of the results. I felt like a large part of my life ended with that DNA test. I wanted a family and parents who wanted me; the type of parents who'd say things like, "I would die for my kids; I'll do anything to protect my children ..." and actually mean it. I wanted parents who would go to the ends of the earth for me. Neither Katrina nor Maurice fit the bill. I felt newly alienated by everyone and everything. I didn't believe Momma's words when she said, "You'll always be family. That test don't mean anything."

But it did mean something—it represented a significant loss I would have to cope with for the rest of my life. It meant I would never have the chance to meet the other person who gave me life. It meant never knowing my history. Without knowing my biological father, I wouldn't know if our facial features or eccentricities matched. Not knowing my real father meant being uninformed about the diseases and health conditions to which I was genetically predisposed. Not having a real, responsible, available, nurturing parent meant a part of me would never be whole. It meant letting go of the dreams I had for Maurice and the ideal father I had imagined in him. Everyone in the world is born with a mother and a father. But not everyone has a Momma and a Daddy. I had a mother and a father. One I knew and wished I didn't; the other, I wished I knew and never would. After the initial conversation, I found it disappointing that no one wanted to talk about the DNA test except me. I wanted to discuss it ad nauseam and to know they were as devastated and irate as I.

Although I believe the DNA results now, I lived in a state of denial for years. I made excuses, and I repeated and retold her story about Maurice having his brother take the DNA test in his place, hoping for it to be true. I continued to blame my mother for his chronic absenteeism. Maybe she had made it too difficult for him to love me.

I also rationalized the DNA results as being part of God's plan for my life. Apparently, God didn't want me to have a father. I told myself lies to make sense of how and why I came into the world to two adults who wanted nothing to do with me. I grieved for the parts of myself I would never know. For how could I ever fully understand myself without ever fully possessing knowledge of the other person who helped to create me? After the DNA results, I was hoping against all hope that some part of Maurice still wanted me to be his daughter. I wish I knew then what I know now: some bonds are meant to be broken. Some parts of our lives are supposed to be left in pieces, so God alone can make us whole.

CHAPTER 21

Birthdays

Every year, my birthday went uncelebrated, and I was used to having my birthday come and go as uneventfully humdrum as Monday mornings because, while growing up under Katrina's roof, we never celebrated birthdays, period. Not Katrina or Darryl's, not Anthony's, and not mine. I often wondered if it were for religious reasons, but never asked.

Birthday parties during my infanthood while living at Momma's house included toys, fanfare, and most importantly cake. We were *supposed* to eat cake in observance—*chocolate* cake. It was my very favorite, but any cake would do. Cake with nuts, fruit, whipped cream; round, square, layered, or Bundt.

I remember seeing pictures of myself wearing a cone-shaped birthday hat and blowing out the candles Momma had placed on my cake. I have other birthday pictures showing my cousins and I at age five sitting next to each other on the swing set happy and carefree. I cherished these pictures as proof that I once lived a celebrated life.

Whatever Katrina and Darryl's beliefs or hang-ups about celebrating birthdays and holidays, birthdays were always special to me. If it weren't for Momma and Maurice sending cards and gifts each year, I wouldn't have ever had anything to demarcate the significance of my birthday from any other day of the year.

On my fourteenth birthday, however, Katrina acted completely out of character by giving me the first birthday present I'd ever received from her. It was Friday, August 13th, 1993. I'd spent the day at home alone, sleeping in and then completing chores and watching TV. Darryl had worked the previous night and returned home at about 7:00 a.m., and Katrina worked most of the day at the beauty shop. I was in my bedroom when I heard her car pull into the garage. She entered through the kitchen and called for me. "Happy Birthday," she said. "I don't know if you like pearls, but here you go."

Placed on the kitchen table was a three-strand pearl necklace, matching stud earrings, and a large, gaudy pearl-and-cubic zirconia brooch. It was unwrapped and was jewelry ill-suited for a teenager like myself. It was something a mature woman three times my age might choose to wear. Next to the jewelry, Katrina had also placed single dollar bills totaling $11. I wondered why she'd dispensed with wrapping the gift if it was truly meant as my birthday gift. Shouldn't it be wrapped up with a pretty bow on top? And why was she giving me back change in cash when she intended this to be a gift?

In fourteen years, she hadn't ever given me any birthday gifts, or ever cared to even mention the words, "Happy Birthday." So, her generosity at this point piqued my curiosity, or rather my skepticism, and got me thinking. I thought, *Why now?* Perhaps, this was a gift she was given by one of her many lovers, and she'd chosen to give me the gift instead of disposing of it? I gave careful consideration to other motivations she may have harbored for the first time.

* * *

Because birthdays weren't celebrated where I lived, every year I looked forward to the days leading up to my birthday when something would arrive in the mail from my extended family, addressed specifically for me. It told me that someone cared enough about me to remember me.

I felt elated to receive something, anything—I didn't care what. Even if what arrived was something I'd never utilize or otherwise wear, I was filled with a sense of gratitude for each and every gift.

To me, birthdays represented my survival, and the prospect of something better in the year ahead. It gave me a reason to hope new hopes and consider new possibilities. In my mind, we are supposed to esteem the miracle of life and celebrate the chance to have a fresh start with each year that passes.

With no observance of birthdays, I was fleeced of any birthday memories to call my own. I wanted to blow out candles and make wishes that may or may not have come true. I wanted one day a year reserved for the expression of joy and laughter. I wanted one day a year to sing Stevie Wonder's version of *Happy Birthday* and sway to the melody. But at Katrina's house, we celebrated exactly nothing. I missed out on the crux of celebratory experiences typically shared by other black families such as cookouts, playing dominos and spades, making raucous jokes with cousins and other extended family, and learning group dances like the *Electric Slide*.

My days were dark, bleak, and hard to manage, but on my birthday, I knew I'd hear from Momma, Maurice, and my aunts. After the paternity results, Maurice continued to send birthday cards. With Katrina's family, on the other hand, I heard the deafening sound of crickets, and I doubted anyone knew the exact date. I diligently saved my birthday cards and compiled them in a growing stack, one on top of the other, in a black shoebox that had formerly belonged to Katrina. I asked her for the box, after I realized I needed a special location to save everything that was meaningful. One of my favorite cards had quarters placed on each side and was decorated with green and pink flowers. The money made the card heavy, and half-circles made an indentation in the red envelope which housed the card and its coins.

Each time I opened the card, I thought about the care it had taken for Momma to place the quarters in each slot and send it to me. Other cards, when I opened them, played a familiar musical tune which made me laugh before closing them quickly. And still other cards surprised me with bright, beautiful 3-D cakes, clowns, and happy birthday notes.

Momma and my aunts always wrote me messages with the date at the top of each card. They signed them "With Love" or "Love Always." At least once a month, I would return to the box, whenever I was feeling particularly low and needed a mental pick-me-up. Reading the cards over and over reminded me that I mattered. Momma's family faithfully sent me cards and letters for St. Patrick's Day, Easter, Halloween, Thanksgiving, and Christmas.

Then one afternoon, when Katina came home in one of her unexplained temperamental rages, she destroyed any concrete evidence I had of ever being significant in the eyes of my family. Finding the box, Katrina grabbed it and taunted me by holding it high over my head. She crushed the sides of the box, as she did so.

"No! No, please," I begged, my throat tightening into a fearful knot. I knew my words would only make her madder, as they escaped from my mouth. My desperate pleas, and the sentiment behind my words mattered nothing to her.

"Since you love your mammy so much, let me show you what I think," she said, her shrill voice hitting a fever pitch. Enraged, her shaking fingers tore to bits every shred of evidence I ever had that others loved me. I could only watch in horror, my mind racing with thoughts of how to reclaim what was being physically destroyed, my face hot and tear-stained. An emotional tidal wave of immense loneliness and emptiness washed over me. *Could I later piece everything back together with tape?* I once again felt helpless and lost as Katrina made me throw the now shredded cards in the garbage. She watched my every move until I came back inside empty-handed. Her violation left me with little reason to live.

"I should have aborted you," she blurted out cynically when I returned. In that moment, as I buried the tatters of my past in the trash, I had to agree with her: death would have been sweeter than enduring the mental games and abuse I was subjected to day in and day out with Katrina. After she spoke those words, I would replay her comment in my head often. I came to think of abortion as an act of love—something she could have done to protect me, but didn't. Knowing she didn't have the capacity within her to love me, perhaps it would have been best if she'd refused to allow anyone to dissuade her from the abortion she claims she wanted.

It was an issue I would later debate in my head, back and forth, until my head hurt. She had other options, yet she chose to carry me to term. She chose to deliver me, give me away, and then go through all the work it took to get me back. She made her own choices and in a morbidly sardonic way, I began to think that her motivation for limiting my contact with Momma, and destroying everything I had of my family in Pine Bluff, was because she wanted me, *right?*

A part of me, the part of me that feels pity for her, understands that she was an emotionally stunted woman who didn't allow herself to inhabit a full range of feelings. And, she didn't understand or ever address the frailty of her mental health. She didn't do the work to understand herself. Instead, whenever she had a bad day, she spread her emotions like a plague—infecting everyone unlucky enough to be around her with her toxicity.

My body felt tired and weary, as I replayed what she'd done. I beat myself up over and over again. I said to myself, *How could you be so stupid? How could you let her find another way to hurt you?* Throughout my life, every time I grew accustomed to each new way she chose to hurt and abuse me (sadly, it became my norm), she always found more cruel ways to inflict pain. I blamed myself for always believing she'd dealt me the worst of it and had reached her capacity, just before it got measurably worse.

I caught myself constantly walking on eggshells and permanently spooked. I skittishly wondered how I might unintentionally trigger her hatred next. Lying in bed, I often prayed, *God I will never, ever forgive her. Get me away from this woman.*

CHAPTER 22

Bodies

"Just look at the butterflies on the ceiling, and it'll be over before you know it," the doctor said. He was tall and Caucasian. He had brown hair and wore a white lab coat. As he examined my breasts, I tried to put on a brave face. When his strange fingers pressed into my skin, I tried to remember this was his job. The examining table felt uncomfortably hard, even with the pillow under my head. I hadn't been prepared to have my feet in stir-ups with my butt at the edge of the table, as if on display. As I looked around the room, I tried to read the posters of anatomical skeletons and found myself lingering on the one giving directions for how to perform a self-mammogram. A cruel cosmic joke, the rooms which housed the worst memories for me always seemed to have white walls. This room had white walls. I wondered if I had something to fear, with this being my first gynecological exam.

He said, "Slide down a little more. You're about to feel my fingers touching you. Do you feel that?"

"Yes," I replied, curtly.

He said, "That's me. Are you okay?"

"Yes."

"Now I'm going to examine your cervix," he said. He directed his nurse to hold the speculum up in the air, so I could see it. "I'm going to use the speculum to help me examine the cervix."

I immediately felt the cold metal tool against my inner thighs and the folds of my vagina. He said, "I'm about to slide two fingers into your vagina and will be using one hand to press on your abdomen. I'm just checking to make sure I don't feel anything abnormal." He kept reminding me to keep my legs spread apart, so he could see.

As he entered my vagina, I thought, *Did I wash enough to mute Mother Nature's odor?* I wondered what he was seeing. And then came the intrusive thought, *I sure hope he's not a pervert.* Fourteen-year-old me wondered how anyone could make the touching of, looking at, and smelling of vaginas their profession. I felt an intense discomfort, as he applied pressure with the examination of his fingers. I continued to stare at the ceiling, and looking at the purple, green, and blue butterflies, I thought, *Are all gynecologists' offices like this?*

As he continued to press on the insides of my vagina with his fingers, he said, "I'm checking your ovaries.

Are you okay?"

I replied, "It hurts, but I'm okay."

The room was uncomfortably quiet. Why didn't they have any soft music playing?

"Now I'm going to swab the inside of your vagina. You're going to feel a little pain."

And as he swabbed from side to side, I clenched my body in anticipation of any additional discomfort. "You're doing well," he said. "We're almost done."

I had started my period four years prior, when I was ten-years old and in the fifth grade. No one had prepared me for the changes. As I sat on the toilet in pain, I'd noticed a red stain on the seat of my panties.

"I need help!" I yelled from the bathroom. "Umm, Ma ...Mom? Something is wrong." The words tumbled out of my mouth. It was the first time I remember giving Katrina a title. Within seconds, she opened the bathroom door. "What? What's wrong with you?" I showed her the blood on the seat of my panties.

"That's your period. You'll be alright." She shut the door, returning a few seconds later with a maxi pad. "Here."

Walking out, she went back into the living room to continue her phone conversation. Laughing, she said, "Girl, she yellin' like she 'bout to die. All she did was start her period." Later, she remarked, "You're a woman now. If you have sex, you can get pregnant."

That's the extent of the sexual education I received as my body matured. Month after month, my cycles

wreaked havoc on me. With a particularly heavy period, I bled through my clothing monthly. The menstrual
blood produced by my body each month flooded, gushed,
and poured out of my small frame. I changed pads every
forty-five minutes to try and prevent bleeding through my
jeans. My period was often prolonged and lasted between
seven days and two weeks. On a few occasions, I bled for
three weeks. In addition to excessive bleeding, I had painful quarter-sized blood clots, mind-numbing headaches,
and excruciating pain in my abdomen, back, and lower
extremities. And although my mother said I was a woman
now, I still felt very much like a child and understood very
little about the mechanics of my reproductive cycle.

I wondered if the pain I felt each month was God's
way of punishing me for the sins I had committed with
Anthony. *Am I being punished for going along, for not speaking
up? Is this a reap-what-you-sow scenario?* I would struggle
with this question often, wondering if the pain I endured
was my curse for being full of sin—God's way of exact-
ing punishment.

After four years of chronic and debilitating cycles, my
mother took me to see the gynecologist. Katrina asked
him, "Can you check to see if she's still a virgin?" Without
answering, he looked at her and then at me. During the
exam, I worried he would tell her the truth. Although
my brother never penetrated my vagina, my body still
felt violated. To me, my brother had taken my virginity,
my purity six years prior. I imagined my genitalia having
some sort of telltale sign. Fourteen-year-old me believed

the doctor would find out my secret. I worried about him telling Katrina.

Speaking to Katrina, the doctor said, "The exam went well. Your daughter is only fourteen, so I don't suspect we'll find anything abnormal when the results come back. I hate to prescribe her birth control pills at such a young age, but it's one way to get the bleeding under control."

Sometime after my first Pap, Katrina questioned me again about being a virgin. My guess is that she'd thought about what her life was like at my age, how she'd given birth by fourteen. Perhaps, she wanted to make sure I didn't end up with the same fate. I chose to believe this was her way of watching out for me. Adding a snarky comment, she said, "You know anybody can tell if you're a virgin. All they gotta do is look for the hymen and see if it's still intact."

I rolled my eyes because I wanted her to quit with the insinuations.

She said, "Has anyone tried to touch you?"

I waited for her to finish probing. How could I tell her what I believed to be the truth: *I haven't been a virgin for a long time.*

She said, "Get your jacket. We're going to Aunt Dorris's."

When we arrived, Aunt Dorris said, "Come on back here and lay down on this table." Aunt Dorris stood next to Katrina, smiling like they were practicing midwives. Smiling as if to say, "We've done this before. Do what we tell you." Feeling as if I were prepping for castration, I laid my bare butt down on the table, parts of me I never imagined a woman—two women—would violate. Unlike the doctor, they didn't ask me how I felt during the intrusion. They did not tell me the next steps or try to protect me from pain. I lay there on a small coffee table with my vagina exposed as they took turns parting my labium.

I noted how ironic it was when they said they just wanted to make sure no one had touched me. Because in that moment, *they* were the ones committing the crime. With my heart beating against the walls of my chest, I thought, *Maybe she knows*. Katrina used her fingers, without gloves or protection, to touch me.

Then Aunt Dorris said, "Move, Kat. Let me see."

Seeing nothing wrong in what she was about to do, Aunt Dorris demonstrated for Katrina how family vaginal exams ought to be performed. It felt like being molested all over again. As they touched my vagina, I stared at the doorway, halfway hoping someone would walk in, halfway hoping no one would see my hairy vagina on the den's coffee table.

After a few minutes, Katrina said, "Put your clothes back on."

She laughed, as I sat up and instructed me to go in the front room.

Feeling like a piece of garbage, I walked out and sat on the couch alone, unable to erase the feeling of their fingers, or the words that were exchanged in the discussion of my body. It became one more thing to profess to

God, not understanding why I had to be subjected to such humiliation.

Without any regard for my personal pride or dignity, Katrina had put my vagina on display and touched me without my consent. By doing so, Katrina reinforced the message that there were no personal boundaries with my body. At any time, anyone could do whatever they wanted.

If I only knew then what I know now: that my body is my own, and no one has rights to it but me. No one gets to touch my body without my consent, not even my mother—not in that way. I wish I could go back and tell my younger self all the truths I know now. Well-meaning family members who claim they are doing this or that thing for your own good have severely misplaced their good intentions and are acting wrongfully. Don't stand for any violations of your body. For years after the home exam, the idea of sexual consent or consensual sex was a foreign one to me. I had no barometer or litmus test to understand what having respect and expecting respect from others meant when it came to my body. I wouldn't understand the power of saying *no* until much later. I thought of my body as having only three functions: sex, pain, and humiliation. When I used to hear people say, "respect yourself," I didn't understand all that was implied. I had no role models of women who could teach me how to cultivate respect for myself, especially not Katrina who was promiscuous from a young age. And Aunt Dorris, whose rigid and strictly faith-based ideas of a woman's ideal conduct, taught me little about how to respect my body in relation to the secular world. I learned the hard way—by discovering what *isn't* respect. I didn't know families weren't supposed to touch each other sexually. I wish someone in my family would have spent time explaining boundaries and appropriate behavior within the context of consent. I now consider my mother's actions at that time, in her complete lack of regard for discerning what was appropriate and what was abhorrently inappropriate, to be a form of sexual abuse.

The physical and sexual abuse I lived through as a little girl resulted in heart-breaking collateral damage as I grew up to become a woman who was obsessed with using my body to please other people at all costs. I figured that if I gave my body to them, they would accept me, like me, and keep me around.

Two years after the degrading home exam, Katrina asked why I didn't yet have a boyfriend at the age of sixteen. My best friend Torrey, who I also had a crush on, asked me, too. High school lunch buddies asked, "Why you ain't wit nobody?" Torrey, who wasn't out to openly hurt my feelings, gave me the derisive nickname *Sneak-a-Freak*. He said with a raised eyebrow, "Quiet girls are the worst ones."

I laughed away the assumptions implicit in their words, as the pressure to be who and what I wasn't mounted on a daily basis. I felt even more out of place, like I was the only kid abstaining from sex and not smoking weed.

While I was on the phone with a classmate one day, she casually said, "My cousin Reggie needs a girlfriend."

"OK," I replied, as if I were performing a community service.

I had some context for who Reggie was. I mainly spoke with Reggie on three-way and four-way lines where five or six people were on the phone at once. We called it a party line. At some point, he and I agreed to meet. I don't remember how it came up, but I told Katrina about him and she responded with genuine interest. "Let me talk to his mother." After they spoke, she agreed we could hang out.

Reggie was a boy who had shiny skin and a complexion similar to mine. He smelled like Dial, the gold bar soap. The detergent-like smell sickened me. It's not that he smelled bad—it's just that the scent was so pungent it would creep into my nostrils and stay there. Even so, there were many things I liked about him. Like the way he towered over my ninety-pound frame and wore starched pants, polo shirts, and clean shoes. He kept his hair clean-cut with fresh waves, and he always had a tight lineup along his hairline. His thick bifocals hung on the tip of his nose. We didn't have much in common at all, except for the time we both posited our opinions about Katrina and her erratic and sometimes crazy behavior. While we were in his room one Saturday, he remarked, "Yo, your mom is crazy. Even my mom said something wasn't right about her."

Getting to know Reggie distracted me by giving me something to think about besides my problems. Once we started dating, I had privileges outside of the house. We spent time at my high school's football games and at his house. He stood a few feet taller than me and had shoulders that were broad and muscular. I always felt secure when he stood behind me, scooping me up in his arms. The top of my head reached his chest line. This kind of intimate security was a much-needed and much-desired first. Kissing him and planning to have sex with him felt like payment for the way he didn't make me feel foolish.

One day he asked me, "Are you a virgin?" When I replied "yes," his giddy excitement was clear even over the phone. In every conversation afterward, he made no secret about what was foremost in his mind, and we talked about what it would feel like to have sex when both of us were virgins. He wondered if I would bleed after the first time. Sadly, I could admit to no one but myself that I didn't want to have sex with him. I just wanted his friendship but didn't quite know how to tell him that. Something in me felt very pressured to give him the thing he had built so much hype around. Unable to ask for what I truly needed from him, I ended up unfairly negotiating with myself by thinking, *If I can't promise him my body, what else do I have?*

"You're my main girl," he would say often enough that I pretended to believe him. His cousin, who was my friend, informed me by saying, "Girl, he's got three girlfriends." The next weekend, I invited him over when I knew we'd have the house all to ourselves. Standing in the living room foyer, he was earnest and said, "Where's your room? I don't have much time." I recalled my brother

Anthony's voice invoking those same words the day he violated me. Hearing my boyfriend repeat these words to me made it clear he had only come over for one reason.

I said, "I don't want to do it in my room. Let's go here." I pointed in the direction of Katrina and Darryl's bedroom. For some reason, it felt too sinful to have sex in my own bed. We wasted no time getting undressed. I knew nothing about foreplay but felt certain there should have been more involved before the actual deed. As he lay on top of me, I felt as if I might suffocate. When he began with quick, full-throttle thrusts, I winced in pain and tried to tell him to slow down, move to the left, take everything out except the tip. He did as I asked, but he didn't ask if I felt okay, or if I wanted to stop. With each thrust, I felt like my insides were splitting in order to accommodate the foreign girth of his penis. Within a few minutes he was done, and I felt a slimy, wet burst inside of me. I pushed him off of me as he collapsed in exhaustion on the floor. His sweaty body lay on the carpet, and he smiled and stared at the ceiling as if he'd just finished playing Game One of the NBA Finals. He'd just played me.

Sitting on the toilet afterward, I wiped away the bright red blood which stained my inner thighs. I was filled with self-regret and thought, *What if he tore something? What if I become pregnant?* By the time I left the bathroom, he'd called his mom to pick him up. There was no post-coital exchange of intimacy. My first time was transactional and loveless.

We talked once or twice afterward, but only because I called him. He first said, "I'm busy." When I continued pressing him to explain why he was ghosting me, he said, "I have another girlfriend." I wasn't surprised, and we never talked again. I had wanted so badly to prove everyone wrong, to prove I could be wanted by someone. Instead, I proved Katrina right. No one wanted me, even after I'd surrendered my body. This mistake became the cornerstone of all of my future relationships.

CHAPTER 23

Things Parents Teach

"Parents still have a big influence on their kids - just ask any therapist. No, really, I think the parent is the most important influence on children: It's how they learn to love and treat other people."

~JUDY BLUME

I counted down the years, and months, and number of days until the end of my sentence living with Katrina. Each birthday signified less time left to serve. My relationship with her felt a lot like the movie *Groundhog Day*: the same fear and the same insanity, over and over again. Still, when I was fourteen, she began teaching me how to drive. She'd tell me, unexpectedly, "It's your turn.

Let's switch."

While I settled into the driver's seat, she'd say, "Seatbelt on?"

Check.

"Check your mirrors, and change them if you need to. Make sure you can see out of all of them."

Check.

"Is your seat comfortable?"

Check.

"Now put your foot on the brake. You remember which one, don't you?" When I had both hands on the steering wheel, she said, "It's more dangerous if you drive with both hands. Try with only one."

When our drive would steer off course, or when I would struggle to get a hold of the wheel or control my rate of speed, Katrina would yell and call me *stupid*. When I accidentally swerved into the opposite lane, without a verbal warning I received a physical rebuke. BAM! She hit me on my face and head several times, punching and slapping any part of my face where her hands landed. It's a miracle I didn't get into an accident. She didn't allow for any mistakes and punished me harshly for mine.

In another punishing memory that I will never forget, one afternoon while I was at her beauty shop, she asked me a question about Darryl. I responded but called him by his government name (*Darryl*) instead of the nickname I'd been taught to use (*Buster*).

Looking up from her appointment book, she said, "What did you say?"

I repeated my reply. She made an aggressive lunge towards me, then retraced her steps and went to the supply closet, picked up a 2x4 board, and hit me over my back with it. She screamed, "Who do you think you are? You ain't grown! You don't get to call him by his first name."

I had never called him by his first name prior to that instance but wanted to know what it felt like—this small act of defiance. No one called him "Darryl," not even his family. Since the day I was introduced to him and instructed to call him *Buster*, something in me didn't want to address him with his nickname. Nicknames were a term of endearment, and I never felt close to him in that way. When we got home, she continued yelling and soon her accusations were in full force. "Are you fucking him? You ain't nothing but a goddamn whore."

I cried and thought about how stupid I'd been and how disrespectful it was to call him by another name when I had no right to do so. Katrina pinned me against the hallway wall and wrapped both bands around my neck, choking me. "I could kill you right now, you fucking bitch."

She punched me twice in the face. The next day, I awoke to two swollen, sticky, black eyes. Part of me felt I deserved it, but the other part of me was completely stunned and in dismay about the reality of my life. I hadn't been the daughter Katrina wanted or needed. I hadn't followed the rules or made any attempt to truly, deeply, seriously bond with her. It was all my fault.

The next day, after seeing the swelling in both of my eyes, she apologized for hitting me and said she would take me to the doctor. Once at the doctor's office, she nervously filled out forms, spoke to the staff, and answered questions on my behalf. I wasn't asked about the injury—not by the receptionist or the medical technician, and not by the nurse or the physician. At each stage of the appointment, she spoke to the professionals privately, asking me to step out of the room. When the physician looked at me, he shook his head, and averting his eyes from my injuries, he told Katrina both of my eyes were infected.

He said, "It's going to take about a week to heal. I'll send the prescription to the pharmacy." Leaving the office, Katrina stood tall as if to protect her pride. She didn't speak, but I understood her message loud and clear: *I'm in charge.* I still can't believe she rationalized such brazen acts of abusive behavior in her own mind. I wish I would have yelled and exposed her, to all the medical staff, "She caused this!" But my fear and silence pervaded the air and reinforced her power's grip over me.

Now as a therapist whose patients are largely children, I understand the high importance of those individuals in helping professions to take the time to be proactive in talking with children who may be suffering in silence. It's important to shed light on ongoing abuse within the child's life as early as possible. Time is of the essence.

CHAPTER 24

Daddy

"You gain strength, courage, and confidence by every experience in which you really stop to look fear in the face. You are able to say to yourself, I lived through this horror. I can take the next thing that comes along."

~ELEANOR ROOSEVELT

Maurice and Katrina kept in touch periodically throughout the years. After moving in with Aunt Dorris and Reva, I wondered if Katrina told him about my exit. As the relationship with Katrina shattered irreparably into tiny shards, my fantasies about rekindling a healthy father-daughter relationship grew into an obsession. My mind was filled with daydreams of us laughing together while on road trips, enjoying bike rides together on warm days, and having him teach me how to change the oil in my car.

While living with Aunt Dorris, I reached out to him for the first time in a long time and dialed his phone number from her bedside phone. As I did so, I was a bundle of nerves, and I got a frog in my throat. This could be the perfect opportunity to build the relationship with him that I'd always wanted. Calling him felt a little like taking the initiative to call my high school crush to ask him out on a date. I grew up in a culture that believed men were the head of their houses and the kings of their castles. Men were endowed with the overall decision-making power in the home. I'd grown up being socialized and taught that men were responsible for making the first move. But this time I made a judgment call about what was in my best interest, and acted first. If I didn't, who would?

When Maurice answered the phone, I said, "Is it okay if I move to Colorado to live with you for a little while?" Unsure of how he would feel about it, I added, "Just for a few months until I leave for the Air Force." I said this comment kind of on the spot, as a way to let him know a plan existed, and that I wouldn't be free-loading. I'd thought about the military but couldn't take action to join until I turned eighteen.

I implicitly understood that a long-term stay wouldn't be welcome. We were on the phone for less than five minutes, but in that time, my heart and mind raced. I thought about all the words I held deep within my heart which would go unsaid. I thought about sharing my dreams of him being my father and me being his daughter. I wanted to tell a family member the full expression of my feelings …to be able to say, "I love you, I love you, I love you" a thousand times. But none of this would ever come to pass.

In the short duration of the phone call, he replied to my question about joining him in Colorado with an apprehensive "yes," but it was still a *yes* all the same! I filled in the drawn-out silences during our phone call with the imagined dialogue I desperately longed to hear: *What happened? Are you okay? Do you need anything? I can't wait to see you! I love you, baby girl.*

Much later, I would realize the intention behind his armored reserve. I would later accept the painful truth that he intentionally kept me at arm's length, not wanting to get my hopes up about where I stood in his life. As soon as we finished speaking, I grabbed the phonebook and called Southwest Airlines to book a one-way ticket to Denver. I ignored my intuition which told me that my daddy-daughter fairy tale was perhaps just the stuff of my dreams.

* * *

Two weeks later, my departure day arrived, and I couldn't believe I would get the chance to spend time with my father. The idea of finally getting to know him sustained me for the interim.

As if I were leaving a bad marriage, I told Aunt Dorris and Reva, "You can give away everything I own. I don't need it anymore."

Everything I owned was tossed into a giant cardboard box. It just reminded me of my abuse, my troubled high school experiences, and my broken family life. Leaving this baggage behind meant I could begin creating a future. Maybe being in Colorado would change my mind about joining the military. Maybe I didn't have to serve in order to escape Katrina. Maybe I could enroll at the University of Denver, live on campus, and join a sorority like Delta Sigma Theta. Maybe I could experience normalcy for the first time in my life! As I prepared for my time with Maurice, I hoped for warmth, hospitality, and new strolls down memory lane.

When I arrived at the Little Rock airport, I looked around neurotically for Katrina, wondering if she'd heard about my plans. I looked over my shoulders, as I progressed through the security lines and made my way to the gate. My insides felt jittery, as I scanned the faces in the airport, thinking about what I would do if Katrina tried to grab me. Thankfully, I made it through airport security and to Denver without interruption. When I arrived, Maurice and his daughter Shan were there to greet me.

We soon arrived at their home, a two-story structure in an orderly, well-maintained, middle-class subdivision. While he carried my suitcase to the upstairs guestroom, I spoke briefly to his girlfriend, Berlinda and the daughter they shared together, Shan. Four years my junior, she was a plump, bright-eyed, quick-witted girl full of energy. I remember my stomach churning with jealousy. She appeared innocent and free and still had a light within her that had long since dimmed in my own life. Her dimpled, exuberant smile revealed she'd been well-loved by her parents. She spoke easily about her favorite shows on Disney and Nickelodeon, most of which I hadn't heard of. She also asked me about my musical taste and who I liked. I grinned as I looked at this kid who was in vogue and up to date with the '90s style.

Shan had the sass I'd lost years ago. I felt diminished and plain stupid in her presence, like I was nothing while she was bestowed with everything. Maurice looked at her as if his world began and ended with her. She was obviously the center around which his life revolved. It was painfully apparent, especially in Shan's presence, that he did not look at me the same way. As he placed his oversized hand on the top of her head, he smiled. I was instantly taken back to that time in my happy childhood when his brother, my Uncle Donny, engaged with me in the exact same way. I remember how loved and how seen I felt in that special moment in time.

I had always loved Maurice's smile, the one he wore in every photo I had of him. He held Shan close to his hip and underneath his arm when they talked. He talked to me without making full eye contact. With her, he shared the details of his day, but with me, he talked about his girlfriend and Shan. He didn't ask about my life, my hopes, or my dreams. He didn't ask about the years he'd missed out on, or how he could help me now with my future. I secretly pined for his conversation and wanted more than anything to get to know him better.

A man of few words, he never shared details about how he'd stood by Katrina's side on the day of my birth. He never once spoke about how his insistence had persuaded Katrina to carry me to term. He also didn't share anything about the day he left Pine Bluff or any of the days that followed. Everything was left to my imagination. I connected the dots where I could. It was weirdly like being with Katrina in that we didn't discuss anything that could have helped me to better understand who I was, and where I hailed from. He just talked, rather insensitively, and without any regard for the current state of my feelings, about Shan, and his girlfriend. He also talked about work.

I told myself, *I get it. I have to accept it. He doesn't love you. He doesn't want you here.* As much as I needed him, I tried to convince myself that I could be strong on my own. I began to ignore the unmet emotional needs of my soul, mind, and heart. What wasn't obvious right away at the time was that I started down a dangerous road of self-neglect and self-endangerment that expressed itself in excessive promiscuity and then later with an attempt to self-injure, which nearly cost me my life. I didn't want to admit to myself what was already apparent. I sometimes consoled myself by saying, *Stop being overly dramatic, it's going to take time for him to get used to you.* In fact, being around Maurice and his family felt like being invited to a birthday party, but spending the day in a corner watching everyone else have fun.

I watched the way Shan tilted her head towards her father as they conversed. She could make him laugh, and I wanted to know her magic. With a complete family unit, she had it all. Maurice, Shan, and Berlinda had *their* life, their way of living perfectly without me. I hated being a witness to their happiness. The part that hurt the most was when Shan called him "Daddy" and knew it to be true.

I taught myself to unravel and forget all the words I had bottled up inside. Words I'd wanted to give voice to, such as, *I love you* and *I need you.* I taught myself to stop begging for his affection. He, in turn, conveniently forgot to tell me how he would still be there for me no matter what, even though we didn't share a real biological connection. He forgot to mention how much he cared about me and missed me. He forgot to tell me how he knew I needed a father figure, and how he wished he could have been there during my most difficult periods. Most painful of all, he forgot to tell me he wanted me to be his daughter, too. Stunned by his choice to remain silent when so much could have been said to bridge the gap between us, I was left feeling defenseless. Living with new sorrow, all the feelings I wanted to express but couldn't find the words to say also went unspoken between us.

Shan and I didn't get the opportunity to know one another well, but my limited engagement with her left me bitter, as I compared my life to hers. She had the bedroom I'd always wanted, with proper girly decorations and toys.

She had privacy and could close her door, talk on the phone, and watch movies without a shroud of constant fear presiding over every thought. She had a best friend and a cousin she often got to visit and spend time with. I envied their closeness. She watched BET and knew the words to Notorious B.I.G.'s song "#!*@ You Tonight." She gyrated and waved her hands to the lyrics. When she asked Maurice for money, clothes, or candy, she got it.

I made my fondest memory of her one day when we were both in the kitchen. She quizzed me on how I made ramen noodles. I told her I added hot sauce. She opened a pack of chicken-flavored ramen, boiled it on the stove, and added hard-boiled eggs, minced onion, lemon pepper seasoning, and hot sauce. This is the only sister memory I have with her. Sitting on the bed in the guest bedroom, I prayed, *God, please keep Shan and I close to one another. I've never had a sister. It hurts to be around her, but please keep us connected.* Looking back, I knew this would never be. Too much envy and the differences in our experiences would forever keep us disconnected. I wanted to be her more than I wanted a relationship with her. A part of me hoped Maurice would grow to love me a fraction of how much he loved Shan. Up until that point, I'd spent my life hoping for the moment he would discover a reason to love me. But real parents don't need a reason to care.

Because of the family's busy schedule, I spent most of my time alone. I had no idea where they were when they weren't home, but they weren't with me. Maurice worked two jobs, and Berlinda stayed busy as an accountant. She often chastised me for not doing chores and for other small things.

Berlinda once burst into my room and said, "You should know better than to leave toothpaste in the sink. And every morning you leave the top off the toothpaste. Don't let me find it that way again." She had one hand on her hip and the other pointed at me. We both knew her anger was fueled by my presence in her home, not by the toothpaste.

From that point on, I retreated into my old ways of trying not to be seen and trying not to be heard. I thought, *If I stay to myself, ask for nothing, and say nothing, maybe she'll forget about me.* I walked on eggshells for a while, afraid of what might happen.

While everyone else stayed busy, I used my time to get to know Maurice and Berlinda by snooping in their belongings. I stared at her ashtray, full to the brim with lipstick-stained cigarette butts. The smell of ashes reminded me of Katrina. Both women were chain smokers who used the sharpness of their words to injure the vulnerable. When Berlina found out I'd rummaged through their private stash of adult videos, she went on the offensive.

Stomping up the stairs, she pushed open the bedroom door and said, "You do not belong in this family. Maurice already has a family with me and his daughter. You aren't his real daughter. You need to pack your stuff and leave. I don't know why you're here."

As my eyes misted with tears, and my face grew hot, I thought, *She's right. What am I doing here?* I wish I had

known then what I know now. Some bonds are meant
to be broken. Some parts of our lives are supposed to be
left in pieces. Some questions don't need answers. I didn't
need to know the truth of how Maurice felt about me.
I had little doubt in my mind she'd uttered those very
words to him before.

Within a day or two, Maurice called from work and
asked me to take a ride with him. He made small talk
about his job and the altitude in Denver, and he also
shared the details regarding a boutique he and Berlinda
were opening. He said, "We thought maybe you could
work there since you don't have anything to do." Starved
for his affection, I immediately began envisioning what it
would be like to help them build the business. He brain-
stormed a few names during the car ride, going through
the motions, as if to make me believe he needed my help.
I sat speechless, trying to figure out what part I would
play—if any. I couldn't remember the last time anyone
had asked for my opinion on anything.

As he parked in front of a small storefront that was located next to a tobacco shop, strip club, and laundromat,
he said, "It's my first store, so I figured I'd name it *Shan's
Boutique*." Although I didn't show how hurt I was at the
time, I couldn't understand how he could be so callous as
to not consider how the name would make me feel. What
I heard in his words were, *I'm going to name my store after my
real daughter.* I felt rejected and disrespected by his idea,
and I wished he'd kept it to himself.

In preparation for the store's grand opening, I helped unpack and hang the items. The store catered mainly to older adults and carried dresses, three-piece suits, and African attire. He worried about the prices of such nice items in a lower-income part of town.

After the store's opening, he spent half the day there while I worked the other half. Business was slow, with people walking in to check it out and quickly walking away after recoiling at prices they deemed to be too expensive. As I sat on a barstool behind the register, I stared at the passersby and made up stories about their lives. I wished someone would stop in and help me pass the time. As *Boney James* played on the overhead speakers, I read the newspaper.

In the classified ads, I spotted a toll-free number advertising a dating chat line. As I picked up the phone, my heart raced. I thought about fake names, and what I could say to keep someone's attention. Calling into the chat line became a daily ritual and every day the men I spoke to provided the entertainment and the break from boredom I needed. I soon became addicted to the thrill of talking to strangers. The conversations always began by asking about age, sex, and location.

I giggled when they said, "Talk dirty to me."

They also said, "What are you wearing?"

When the men ended the call after I truthfully described my striped tank top, khaki shorts, and white Nikes, I learned to respond by saying, "A small T-shirt and panties." After a short intro, they always asked to meet. When I told them I lived with my dad and didn't have a car, they responded like dogs in heat: "No problem. Just send the address."

One such man was a Marine with blonde hair. At 6'3" and 240 pounds, he dwarfed me. He picked me up and drove me an hour away to his home in Boulder. During the drive, I asked myself how I would be remembered, as I mentally prepared myself for the chance he might rape me and dispose of my body. No one would know about my whereabouts. The drive seemed to go on forever, as he talked about his job and having little time to meet anyone. We arrived at his home in the woods, a cabin-like structure with floor-to-ceiling glass windows and reclaimed wooden beams. I gave in to the idea that I might not go home, and wondered how I could have been so stupid, so irresponsible, and so desperate. But I found him to be quite nice and considerate when he asked several times if I needed anything to drink or eat. He wanted to make sure I knew he didn't have an STD, and afterwards he asked how I felt. During the time in his home, I became muted and afraid, a stark difference from the outgoing girl he met over the phone.

Another one of the men I met via the chat line was a police officer who was biracial—Hispanic and Native American— he loved his job and spent hours talking to me about his work patrolling the highways. As he took me on a tour of his apartment and showed me photos of himself and his family, he asked to see me more. It was a request I couldn't understand. Why would he want to

spend time with a teenager who couldn't offer any conversation in response to his lived experiences? I treated
my body like it was a greasy cheeseburger in the bottom
of a paper bag, given to my lovers at a drive-through
window with a receipt that said, *Eat me*. I hated myself for
the way I gave my body away. It would take a long time,
and meeting the love of my life, before my lost sense of
self-respect was restored.

CHAPTER 25

Worn-Out Welcome

While I was working alone at the store one night, Berlinda, taking drags from her cigarette, clamored through the door ahead of Maurice. "I told you that you ain't got no business in our bedroom. You've been snooping around our stuff again!" Maurice caught her, as she lunged at me with her fist and tackled her to the ground. They argued, and Maurice forced her outside. The next day, he told me to pack my bags. "You can't stay with us; it's causing too much conflict. I have another place." He moved me about a mile up the road to another two-story home, a rental property. He purchased furniture and installed cable.

When I wasn't working in the store, I thought about my next steps. After Belinda made it quite clear how I'd

overstayed my welcome, I looked up and contacted the
Air Force recruiting office. During my weeks of preparation to join the Air Force, an unexpected delivery arrived
in the mail from Arkansas. Katrina had sent a crumpled
box with all of my childhood photos, clothing, and other
miscellaneous items. I picked up each item carefully; the
picture frames which held my fifth and sixth grade photos
were shattered. Shards of glass were mixed in with all of
my belongings. She included a note: *I am sending the rest of
your money to you. I have deducted $500 from your savings ac-
count for living expenses.* She listed amounts for rent, water,
electricity, and gas. I felt a biting sarcasm I'd never felt towards her. Her handwritten tally of living expenses made
me chuckle, as it re-confirmed she had never viewed me
one bit as her daughter.

The Air Force recruiter and I set a time to meet,
and he agreed to come to the house since I didn't have
transportation. After the recruiter received my high
school diploma and social security card, we met several
more times to finalize the paperwork. I made one of the
most important and serious decisions of my life all alone.
Maurice, Shan, and Berlinda were absent as I partici-
pated in the Air Force's swearing-in ceremony. Seven
months had come and gone. I had taken no pictures with
my new family, and had no stories to tell about my time in
Colorado. I was no closer to building a relationship with
Maurice than I had been the first day I arrived.

Two days after Christmas, in the middle of a snow-
storm, the Air Force recruiter met me in the driveway of

Maurice's home. Earlier in the day Maurice had picked me up from his other home, possibly so that I could say one last *goodbye* to him and his family. As I'd expected, by that point, very little was exchanged in the way of intimacy, and after a stiff sideways hug, Maurice and I parted ways, as I opened the vehicle door.

CHAPTER 26

Dream

I like having the ability to take my dreams as far and wide as my imagination will go. I like envisioning a better world than the one that already exists. I also like how the mind can move backwards and forwards in time. It's why I fell in love with books at an early age. Reading helped me to imagine not just how each character lived, but how I could live. Imagination led me to writing, and writing ushered me through healing. The quest for healing led me to where I am today.

When I think about the fathers in my life, three exist. The first is God, my creator and my salvation. The second is the one named on my birth certificate, Maurice. The third is my real father who represents the other half of my biology, yet someone who I will most likely never meet or know. If God had given me a choice, I would have preferred a deadbeat biological father to an unknown biological father. I would have preferred to know the lineage of my real father's family. I would have liked to have known something about the man whose DNA I share. Instead, my mind is littered with memories of a man I loved who is not related to me and who does not desire to be in my life.

Countless times, I've imagined how my world would be if I knew my real father. What does he look like, and do we resemble one another? I have often dreamed of a man whose milk chocolate complexion and sparkling teeth radiate throughout the room. I picture him with a perfectly shaped Afro, a goatee, and broad shoulders. He would look like a member of the Black Panther party, ready to defend his people. In my dreams, we share the same warm eyes. He's a quick-witted jokester with a hearty laugh. He's protective, compassionate, and affectionate, like me. He is also resilient, a brave lion who has humble strength and stands tall in the face of turbulence. He takes his space in the world seriously, and pledges to leave people better than he found them. My real father is a man who puts his family first. If he knew me, he would love me unconditionally and cherish me as his own.

I believe that the best parts of who I am came from God and a man I'll never know. For sanity's sake, I must imagine a better man. I cannot live and die believing the two halves of me are solely the parents I've already met. I cannot live with the thought that my biological father is another man who would not want me. The absence of my father has left me empty, damaged, lonely, and constantly questioning. I dream of a man who would love me in all the ways Maurice did not. To my real father, wherever you are—thank you.

CHAPTER 27

Fly High

"He who conceals his disease cannot expect to be cured."
~ETHIOPIAN PROVERB

I grew up loving fairytales and nursery rhymes. I enjoyed reading about characters overcoming obstacles, falling in love, and conquering foes while coming out victorious and winning at the end. In the story of *The Three Little Pigs*, the Big Bad Wolf went to the first house, which was made of straw, and he blew it down. He went to the second house, which was made of sticks, and he blew that one down, too. Lastly, he came to the sturdiest home, the one built of bricks. He attempted to blow it down but couldn't. When I was a child, the story of the pigs and the predatory wolf reminded me of my relationship with Katrina. She threatened each home I lived in. She chased, huffed, and puffed until she ripped and destroyed parts of me. Like the little pigs, each home I left represented a chance to flee. At one time, the military had felt like the safe house, a place where I could relax, knowing she couldn't hurt me even if she tried.

Self-preservation drew me to join the Armed Forces. When I was on my way to class during high school, I had zipped past the cafeteria, where two Air Force recruiters stood in front of a folding table with pamphlets and business cards. I didn't stop to speak to them, but I committed the idea to memory. I looked forward to seeing the world and its people differently—better—than what I had experienced in Arkansas. I had no expectations or preconceived notions about what it would be like to call myself an *airman*. I hadn't worried about whether military life would be a good fit. I just knew it would offer one thing, the most precious thing: a chance to escape. Most of the people I met had prepared for the military by eating healthy, working out, cutting their hair, and rehearsing the reason they wanted to serve their country. Not me. I gave zero thought to the fact that I'd never done one push up or run a lap.

No one could have prepared me for Basic Training, the stepping-stone that acclimated new members to military culture. It was designed to physically and mentally prepare recruits for active duty. We were supposed to strip ourselves of individuality and replace it with team cohesion and uniformity. During the six weeks of Basic Training, we learned discipline, accountability, and loyalty to the military. We were taught military history, customs, and courtesies—and later tested on the same. Like a team of AI robots, we were trained to be mission-focused, operationally minded, and ready to deploy at any moment. For our entire military career, this lesson permeated what, when, and how we operated. Core values and the Airmen's Creed were recited proudly and with *oomph*. Regardless of gender or assignment, we were all airmen.

When you're in the military, the job takes precedence to everything else. Your personal life takes a back seat and will, for no reason, ever impede the mission. When I was in the military, there was no time to unpack and process the traumatic stress of my past.

While I tried to retain and regurgitate all the new information I learned, being invited to join the military and then being accepted was like being asked to adopt a whole new way of living with new standards and new expectations. I found myself feeling underprepared for the opportunity to become an adult within this new context. I was afraid of failure, and self-deprecating thoughts ran endlessly on a hamster wheel in my mind. *What if I don't pass my PT test? What if I'm not military material? What if ...?* Everyone else seemed to be starting at lap one, while I was a hundred yards behind. I don't know if anyone noticed, but I always felt like I was trying to catch up. Each week, I did the best I could while counting down the weeks until graduation. With military life came a schedule that didn't allow too much time for reflecting on my troubled past. At first this was a good thing. Instead of speaking to the elephants in my life, I colored them invisible. For the time being, I adapted and overcame.

Still, the experience of surviving my first year in the military felt like *hell week* every single week. The memory problems I had experienced in school continued during Basic Training. I didn't have any coordination, either. When everyone else started marching with their left foot, I started with my right, tripping and stumbling the whole way. A trio of girls in my flight laughed and pointed at my short, matted hair and ashen skin, as they stood a safe and removed distance away.

As everyone else slept, I tossed and turned until night became morning. On nights when I managed to get a couple of hours of sleep, I always awoke out of breath and in a cold sweat from nightmares. I often had flashbacks to my Arkansas pain. And I couldn't stop thinking about how wrong and unfortunate my experience had been with Maurice, and my time in Colorado. I blamed myself for everything. When the thoughts came, they enveloped me. I tried to push them to the back of my mind—sometimes it worked, most times it didn't.

I couldn't seem to shake the insecure feeling that I was too broken to be what the military needed me to be. I weighed less than one-hundred pounds and dealt with frequent headaches, stomach aches, nausea, and lack of appetite. During a military physical, the kind doctor, who was taken aback by my frail frame, recommended an increase in fiber to prevent constipation. Speaking in a motherly tone, with soft eyes hidden behind her glasses, she instructed me to hide pieces of bread and fruit in my pockets. The training instructors in basic training didn't allow us to take food or snacks with us. During the six weeks of training, I experienced exhaustion, panic attacks, and crying spells.

With vacant eyes and slumped shoulders, I walked around thinking of myself as a failure. The intrusive thoughts undermined any sense of accomplishment. *What am I doing here? I'm not military material.* No matter how I felt on the inside, a plan B didn't exist. At night, with my heart thudding against my chest, I feared the instructors would walk in and tell me to pack my bags. *Where would I go?*

Weekends, however, provided me with some much-needed rejuvenation. I had time to shop, call Momma, and find my way back to Jesus. I and hundreds of other trainees attended the Sunday service at the chapel. Unsure of what to pray, I whispered, *God, help.*

After six weeks, the Boot Camp graduation felt anti-climactic. Everyone except me walked around exuberant, in a celebratory mood. We'd survived Basic Training. My insecurities were nursed by the other airmen's camaraderie, as they sat on their bunks and chattered with one another about who would be attending the graduation to support them. After the ceremony, the airmen's family members ran up with floral bouquets and balloons to greet and embrace them. I remember walking alone after

the conclusion of the ceremony in my military-blue uniform, thinking of my family, and how I wished Momma,
Aunt Yolanda, and all my aunts could be there to see me.

I continued my training in San Antonio at technical
school, and I was assigned to the Logistics Readiness field
for six more weeks. Technical school operated like Basic
Training, but with more independence. Instead of sharing
open barracks with forty other females, I shared a room
with just one. On weekends, we were allowed to visit family, attend parties, and act somewhat like adults. After
acclimating, I met some people around my age who had
found a way to sneak alcohol into the dorm. And at clubs,
I met a variety of men, young and old. Self-medicating
the loneliness with alcohol and sex soon followed. I had
no clue as to how people formed healthy friendships, but
I knew how to offer my body.

After graduation, I received orders to Mountain
Home Air Force Base in Idaho. I wondered if being so
close to Colorado would be good for me. When I arrived
at the airport in Boise, I waited more than an hour for my
sponsor to arrive. Sponsors are like welcome committee
members and virtual assistants all in one. They assist military members with acclimating to their new assignment
by assisting with housing, providing tours of the military
base and city, introducing the member to important
people, and being available for questions and assistance.
Overall, they help the military member to have a smooth
transition. Using a payphone near baggage claim, I called
my duty section. The first sergeant answered and said,

"We are so sorry. We forgot you were arriving today. Your sponsor is on leave. We don't have anyone who can pick you up. You'll have to catch a cab. We'll see you when you get here. Tell the driver to drop you off at billeting."

A white woman in her fifties with frizzy gray hair said, "It's going to take me an hour to get there, and I charge $100."

I thought, *Why me?*

She made me show her my money before she would agree to drive me to the Air Force base. She talked to me the way someone asks for money before performing a service when they think they will be scammed. Sitting in the front seat, I fought back tears, as she tried to make small talk.

I thought, *Why can't anyone remember me? Is this what the rest of my life will look like—alone?*

As the days and months passed, I tried my best to act like a strong military member. I watched people and took mental notes on how to interact. I tried to mimic a good airman by learning to march, making appropriate eye contact, standing erect, and walking on the right side of the hallway with my arms straight against my side. But sadness continued to swallow me whole, and often ambushed me in the most banal moments, like when I was walking down a grocery store aisle. I would have traumatic flashbacks, while I stood in the snack aisle selecting which flavor of Doritos I wanted. Sadness would come while I was listening to music that was meant to make me feel good, like Prince, Whitney Houston, or New

Edition. Sadness also came while I was at work training to learn my job. All of a sudden I would think, *I hate myself. I shouldn't be here.*

During my annual physical examinations, the doctor always asked, "Do you have problems sleeping?"

I always said, "No Sir/Ma'am."

"Do you feel depressed or have feelings of suicide or homicide?"

"No Sir/Ma'am."

We grow up being told honesty is the best policy, but we're also told not to air our dirty laundry. Even the military sends mixed messages on how honest we should be. When no Plan B exists, lying is the best policy. I feared being labeled unfit and later discharged if I answered honestly. My entire chain of command would know about my mental state; privacy and confidentiality are neither a right nor a guarantee when you're government property.

In the military, faking became a way to survive. Asking for help looked good in a counseling pamphlet but didn't translate to the real world. I understood early that the military wasn't designed to manage pre-existing trauma, and everyone I knew wore an invisible mask and towed the line.

What confused me most about the military is how we branded ourselves as family. By some stretch of the definition, maybe we were, so long as we conducted ourselves in concert with the other members—so long as we looked, acted, and sounded the part. I had made faulty assumptions prior to my joining. I'd thought that when I got into the military, I'd meet surrogates who would be my mother, aunts, and best friends. But in a patriarchal majority where few women held leadership positions, few could be trusted as a friend and confidant. Our focus centered on winning awards, gaining recognition, and being promoted to the next rank. Everyone else tried to be ready for the mission, ready for the next assignment, ready for the next rank—while I tried to be normal. Ignorantly, I thought I could replace my dysfunctional family by creating a new little family from the people I met. But if the Air Force was my family, it was one I would have to remain as closely guarded with as the one I'd left. Acknowledging what I knew to be true about my mental and emotional health could have been a catalyst for losing the life I'd worked hard to obtain. I'd lose my friends, income, independence, even my home. Pretending and denying were behaviors I'd learned well before joining the military. The military's treatment of people with mental illness discouraged many from seeking help. My issues were rooted in generations of family secrets. *What goes on in this house stays in this house.*

CHAPTER 28

Closure

While sitting on the twin-sized bed in my dorm room at Mountain Home Air Force Base, Idaho, I opened my window to see the airmen who were out and about. A few months had passed since I'd left Colorado, but staying so busy in the Air Force had kept me from too much reminiscing. That morning, everyone was cleaning, making Saturday night plans, or just waking up. It was one of those days when people washed cars, had yard sales, or went to the park. As I watched my dorm-mates taking advantage of the spring weather, I built up the nerve to call Maurice. To prevent myself from getting distracted during the conversation, I turned off the *Golden Girls* marathon that was playing on television. Needing closure, I dialed his number on my cell. I knew what I wanted to say, but I wasn't sure if it would come out as intended.

My nerves were getting the best of me, as I listened to each ring. A part of me hoped he wouldn't pick up the phone. He answered, and after the customary greeting, I got straight to the point. Speaking in the most calm and assertive tone I could muster, I said, "As a little girl, I remember sleeping in the bed with you before you got up to leave. I heard you tell Momma you were heading to Colorado. Why didn't you stay in contact with me?"

I'd replayed the memory at least a thousand times. I knew that if it weren't for me going to him, he wouldn't have said *goodbye*. If it weren't for me asking to live with him after I graduated from high school, he wouldn't have been a part of my life at all.

After a short pause, he replied, "Well, at the time, Berlinda was pregnant, and she gave me an ultimatum. Either choose you or her, otherwise she would leave me."

As he spoke, I held my hand over my mouth, so that he would not hear me cry. It was the first time he had spoken to me openly. Pausing and taking a deep breath, I thanked him for being honest before ending the call. He had confirmed what I'd always speculated about our relationship.

I reflected on the ways he had tried to care for me, even superficially. Even with Berlinda's disapproval. The DNA results may have stood as an answered prayer for their family, and a chance to close an inconvenient door. My presence and my neediness did not fit into their ready-made family life. Maurice had cared for me as much and for as long as he could. He didn't express the capacity for more.

Suddenly, I no longer felt comfortable asking him to be my daddy. I was done begging him to be anything. It was time to pick up the pieces of my heart he'd left behind, and realize I could make it without him. In fact, I already had. I vividly remember sitting with my legs folded in front of me and crying after the call. I didn't shower or eat, as I grieved the loss of someone who had once meant everything to me. I stayed in my room for the rest of the day, unsure of how to proceed. How would I move on without family? I said to myself, "You can do this. You have been through much worse." That weekend, I mourned what I'd never had while also giving myself a pep talk. *Now you know the truth! Don't call him anymore. Don't ask him for anything. Grow up, act like an adult, and move on!*

CHAPTER 29

Forgiveness

*"Train up a child in the way he should go; even when he is old
he will not depart from it."*

~PROVERBS 22:6 (NKJV)

During my first two or three years of military life, I
attended church regularly. Not going felt like backsliding,
which the church often spoke about. Being new to making
my own decisions, I chose to attend non-denominational
churches. I wanted to separate myself from labels such as
Missionary Baptist and *Pentecostal Holiness.* My upbringing
had convinced me that denominations and man-made
labels did little as far as my relationship with God. On
Sundays, I couldn't seem to get rid of the shame from my

childhood and the guilt over distancing myself from my biological family. Shame prevented me from attending on a regular basis. Leaving and choosing to cut ties felt like an act of rebellion at times, and at other times like living life on the run.

There were moments when I created a new self-deprecating narrative to explain my unstable upbringing. I blamed myself for the distance I experienced between myself and my family. I blamed myself for not being the good, well-behaved child Katrina deserved. I rationalized her behavior by casting her as an imperfect parent with an overly-sensitive, oddball child. For a brief time, I believed we could slowly build a bridge toward understanding each other. The more I listened to friends discuss their relationships with their parents, the more I craved the same. I wanted someone, anyone, to care about my day and worry about my safety and well-being.

I called her a few times, and even provided Katrina with my phone number and address, and guardedly gave her insight into my life and relationships. I tried to create the mother-daughter relationship I'd always wanted by sharing mundane details about military life and reminiscing about music we both enjoyed. I thought sharing a fraction of myself could turn into something meaningful beyond what I already knew to be true. I'd never confided in her for any reason, but I would never know if my memories of her were real unless I gave her a second chance.

So, the day before my twentieth birthday, I called her. I hoped for a "Happy Birthday" wish, but her voice sounded groggy and lethargic as she said, "Your birthday should be coming up sometime this week, shouldn't it?"

That was not what I'd expected or hoped she would say. Her comment reminded me of every birthday we hadn't celebrated in the past and how meaningless they'd all felt. Flatly, I said, "Yes." She said something like, "I hope you enjoy your day."

I fumed inside because she'd failed my test. How could a woman forget the date she gave birth? I swore to myself I would never speak to her again, and I distanced myself without telling her why. I called Sprint and changed my number that day. I pledged to no longer have any contact with Katrina. She would not receive an explanation for the reason. This would be *goodbye* forever.

* * *

Maybe she worried after being cut off. Maybe it angered her—after all, she was my mother. Sometime afterward, while I was working in the Transportation Maintenance Operations squadron, the first sergeant, Master Sergeant Seiler, asked that I step aside, so he could speak to me.

"Someone called and stated she's your aunt. She said you need to get home because your mother has cancer."

I shook my head and said, "It's not true."

With a puzzled look on his face, he said, "Do you need to take some time to think? The person on the other end sounded concerned."

Looking him in the eye, I replied, "My mother is sick and has mental issues, but she doesn't have cancer."

If it were true, I might actually sleep better knowing she would never hurt me again. I thought about how I would feel after being notified of her funeral. *Would I attend? Would I speak if asked? What would I say? Am I making a mistake by assuming she's lying?* All these thoughts flooded my mind, as I tried to protect myself.

According to Master Sergeant Seiler, the family member had begged for me to return the call by saying, "She's in the hospital asking for you. She has cancer." But I knew it was an elaborate hoax. Intuition rarely fails us and creating a fictionalized account of her impending death was just another way for Katrina to mess with my head. She was nowhere near death's door, and I knew it. I didn't fall for the trick, and took no unnecessary time off from work.

* * *

Another year passed at work with no further incident. I hoped Katrina would accept the distance I placed between us. In all honesty, I hoped she would erase all memory of me. I'd changed jobs and relocated to North Carolina; I felt good about my new beginning as a Health Services Administrator in the 4th Medical Group. I cross-trained from my job in Logistics to gain experience working with people in the medical field. At the rank of E-5, I supervised five airmen who worked at the clinic's front desk and in the medical records department. My superintendent, Senior Master Sergeant Owens, a man in his late forties with a witty sense of humor, motioned for me to follow him into an exam room. "You might want to have a seat." With a rolled piece of paper in his hand, he pointed towards the exam table that sat in the center of the small room. In a solemn tone, he said, "Please sit down. The Red Cross called. Your mother passed away."

I replied, "No, she hasn't, and I'm certain of that." I gave him a fifteen-minute explanation of my complicated history with a mother who's recently started to act out in desperate and inappropriate ways to drag me back into the madness of her world.

Within my military records was documentation saying I did not want to be informed if Katrina or Maurice attempted to contact me for any reason. I placed notes in the margins of emergency contact forms, life insurance forms, and anything else that required me to list my parents' names. I needed anyone who might touch my file to know that I did not come from the type of family most people could call in case of emergencies. But I didn't know for sure if my written requests raised eyebrows, since I never completed or reviewed the paperwork in the presence of the people who would ultimately handle it. No one ever called me to ask for clarification. In the section asking me to list the name of my father, I added, "I don't know." That part felt like a lie even to me because Maurice had been my father in my heart for most of my life.

Senior Master Sergeant Owens immediately contacted the Red Cross and, based on his conversation with the
Red Cross, they shared with him the details of the call.
According to what he'd been told, the call center spoke to
a woman who identified herself as being in Arkansas and
a member of my family. She told the Red Cross volunteer
my mother had passed. The volunteer stated quite sin-
cerely that she'd seen the notes pertaining to my parents
but felt pressure to at least try to notify me of the death.
As time passed after Katrina's forceful and deceptive
intrusion into my life, I again dug my way back from the
fear and shame she'd instilled in me as a child. Over the
course of the next few months and years, I focused my
attention on praying for God to change my heart about
her. *Afterall, she's still my mother.* I still didn't want a relationship, but I did want to know what freedom felt like.
What would my life feel like if I harbored no feeling at all
towards her? I would do anything to be free.

* * *

If being a Christian and regularly attending church
had reinforced anything, it was that nothing would work
unless I attempted to forgive. I became captivated by
listening to Joyce Meyer, an evangelist and author with
a strong, commanding Southern voice. She spoke with
authority. Every day, every sermon, I watched and took
notes. She discussed her upbringing and being abused by
her father, until she left home at eighteen. Joyce shared

the fear and disappointment she felt due to living with an abusive father. She also testified about how her mother knew of the abuse but refused to protect her. Joyce spent many years learning how to let go of the past and forgive her parents. She prayed, ministered to, and cared for both parents when they became incapacitated. Both parents sought her forgiveness and accepted Christ into their lives. Our stories differed, but the pain of being abused and having family turn a blind eye felt similar.

Joyce's matter-of-fact tone when she used the word "rape" instead of sexual abuse gave me permission to be honest about my own history of sexual violence, coercion, and beatings. In telling her own story, she also told mine. She allowed me to acknowledge parts of my story I'd hidden, and other parts I didn't know existed. As a child, I didn't have the vocabulary to acknowledge my feelings of shame, remorse, and embarrassment. She helped me forgive myself for self-medicating my pain in self-destructive ways. I considered her to be my life teacher and role model. Without her, I wouldn't have understood the concept of forgiveness. She often said, "Forgiveness isn't for them, it's for you." I believed her. She also said, "You pray for them to be blessed, and when you pray, God will show them what areas need repentance. And if they have a need, you bless them."

When I wasn't listening to Joyce Meyer, however, I awakened with the same story, same hurt feelings, same reasons to be angry. I got tired of carrying the weight of my childhood—the times I believed God had screwed me.

I couldn't shake the thoughts of how spiritually deserted and parentless I felt when Katrina masked her abuse as discipline. I'd successfully gotten away from her, by putting as much physical distance between us as possible, so why couldn't I get over it and move on with my life? Why couldn't I just be happy, whatever that meant?

Sometimes when I called my Arkansas family members, they'd say in their half-hearted, sympathetic tone, "Girl, you gotta let it go." They'd also remind me, "Katrina's still your mother. You have to forgive." Their words struck me as being dismissive and placed me back in the time when I had been victimized by my own mother. Stupidly, I hoped that as an adult I could speak to Momma and my aunts as a grown woman, seeking counsel and understanding from other grown woman. I hoped that they would understand my plight. Instead, I learned my most sensitive, battered parts couldn't be shared, and the family who I longed to heal me could not be trusted.

I've heard Joyce say, "Unforgiveness is like drinking poison and wanting the other person to die." I didn't want to die, at least not from that. Needing answers, I read Ephesians 6:2-3: "Honor thy father and mother; which is the first commandment with promise. That it may be well with thee, and thou mayest live long on the earth." How could I honor the one who first dishonored me? How could I honor parents who did not treat me as a child in need of love, security, and validation?

Four years after leaving home, I decided to take a small but significant step to ushering in my own healing process, which was long overdue. Sitting in my car one afternoon, I thought about what I wanted to say to my mother. When I arrived home, I wrote, "I forgive you for what you did and didn't do in my life." I tried to explain that I knew Katrina had done the best she knew how. As delicately and forthrightly at possible, I jotted down my desires to move forward. I said something like, "Maybe we can grow to be friends." I was anxious and struggled to come up with the right words. Reading the almost two-page letter, I wondered if I made sense. Would she feel my sincerity? I wanted my letter to come across as intelligent and compassionate. With nervousness inhabiting the pit of my belly, I prayed, *God please let my words be received in the way they are intended.* I placed it in the mailbox and hoped for the best. Still, I couldn't forget the Katrina I'd left a few years prior.

However, she might respond, at least I could say, "I've done my part." I knew my step of good faith would have to be enough. I wanted the type of mom I could call daily to say, "I love you" or "I hope you have a good day." *God help me forget the past.* I wanted a mom I could sit in a room with while still feeling comfortable in my skin. *God, take all the memories and make them disappear.* I wanted a mom.

During my early twenties, I found myself always being the only person within my group of acquaintances who had little to no strong family connections. I would never get used to the loneliness and isolation. I would never know what it was like to go on family vacations, attend anniversary and birthday parties, or go to Mom and Dad's house for the holidays. I would never know what it felt like to sit in the kitchen together, share inside jokes via group text, or take pictures wearing matching pajamas. I could only imagine the joy other people felt as sisters and cousins attended one another's weddings and baby showers. I could only imagine what it felt like to hold newly born nieces and nephews. My family stories could never be told in ways that make people cry from laughing.

Wanting a family and craving connection is normal and OKAY. Having a family is no little thing; it's huge, beautiful, and unattainable for some of us. Every person deserves to live with people they love and who love them in return. That is why I wrote the letter, and that is why I wanted to forgive Katrina.

Maybe two to three years after I sent Katrina an olive branch, I received a response. While on my lunch break, I checked the mailbox and saw a letter with a stamped postmarked that read "Little Rock, AR." I scanned the envelope and noted it didn't contain the sender's name or postal address. I opened the letter with caution, knowing the sender could only be one person. I readied myself for the tsunami that was about to destroy my military home, taking with it my sense of safety and robbing me of the privacy I had worked hard to establish.

She wrote, "I'm finally getting the chance to respond. You think you're so smart. I've thought long and hard about the letter you sent. I reread it every day. I couldn't sleep from reading your words. You thought you could change your number, move, hide from me. You can't

get away from me. I have your social security number; I
can find you."

Reading the letter, I froze in fear and disbelief at what
I sensed would follow. She wrote, "I don't have anything
to be forgiven for. I didn't do anything wrong. You are the
one who needs help. You have always been a pathological
liar and a problem child."

That was the Katrina I'd known my whole life. In an
instant, she had sent me back to being that eight-year-old
child who was beaten in the living room of our downstairs apartment.

Soon after, she executed various ways of getting her
point across. As I entered my apartment after work, I
saw the red message indicator light of my cordless phone
blinking in my bedroom. Pressing play, the familiarity
of her voice shook me: "You can't get away from me. I
am your mother. You ain't nothing but a black bitch. I
hate the day I gave birth to you. I should have aborted
you when I had the chance." She ended the message by
saying, "If I ever see you again, I will kill you."

In an instant, I remembered how she had made it
impossible for me to feel safe telling people about the
abuse when I was a child. She raised me away from the
only family I had ever loved and made me vulnerable to
her abuse—I was an easy target. I was too afraid to tell
anyone during childhood, and, alienated from my family as an adult, who could I tell now? Having no shelter
and no support system, I sat alone in my living room,
paranoid and afraid. I wondered if she were outside my

apartment ready to make a rude re-entry into my life. I felt imprisoned at the thought of her destroying all I'd worked so hard to create. What if she had hired someone, like a private eye, to watch me? My thinking turned into toxic paranoia, and I went as far as to think, *What if she hatches a plan to murder me?*

For months and years, tears streamed down my face each time I thought about her message. I tried to tell myself, *I am no longer that little girl from Arkansas. I'm grown now.* I tried to walk taller, tell myself anything, so I wouldn't feel impotent. Before her threats, I had never imagined I might actually have to save my own life by defending myself against her. I'd never thought of having to take anyone's life before. If worst came to absolute worst, how would I live with myself if I killed my mother in a desperate act of self-defense?

Within the next few weeks, while I was working at the medical clinic's triage line, I heard from Katrina again. Sitting in the darkened room with a female active duty nurse to my left, I took call after call from patients in need of appointments, lab results, and referrals to specialists. I recognized one voice immediately. "You can't get away from me. I am your mother. I'm the one who called the Red Cross. I will always find you. You think you hurt me by writing that letter. You didn't. You hurt yourself."

For a few seconds, I allowed my silence to speak for me. I didn't want to give her any indication that she'd rattled me. Sitting upright in my chair, glaring at the computer screen, I said, "Nice to speak to you, Katrina.

Is that all you needed?" I addressed her as if she were any other patient on the line for fear of being unprofessional and causing the nurse, who was an officer, to be alarmed.

Speaking in the same cold, measured, harsh tone as in my childhood, she said, "I read your letter. I kept it on my desk and stewed over it. You *forgive* me for what *I did and didn't do*, huh? Yeah, I had to figure out how to respond, so it's taken me a while. You thought when you left you could get away from me, but you can't. I know people in the military who will give me any information I need. Make sure you keep up payments on your apartment and car. You have a nice car, by the way. I know everything about you. I can come to North Carolina any time I get ready. I have your address."

I ended the call afraid, more afraid that I had been in a long time. I was unsure of how to defend myself and regain my safety. A part of me wished I could have outsmarted her by drowning her in words I didn't mean: "I love you, and may God bless you—Mom." The other part of me wanted to give it to her like she gave it to me: "I hope you die a lonely, miserable death. You are the worst mother I've ever known." I wanted to defend myself and take away the smirk I imagined she wore, but I felt choked. I wanted to remind her of what it means to be a real mom, remind her how mothers encourage their children, wipe away tears, and do kind gestures to make their children smile. She'd done the opposite. I considered her to be the *anti-mother*. Whatever hope I had of us being like Dorothy and Sophia on the *Golden Girls* evaporated in the wind.

CHAPTER 30

Finding Grace

Katrina must have been so fearful at the thought of losing me. I would also guess that my mother was a lonely woman. Loneliness in and of itself can make us behave in ways we would not, if we felt we had any other choice. How could she explain my absence? For a woman who always needed to be in control, how could she explain losing a person she had brought into the world? The phone calls snatched me back to feeling like a defenseless little girl. It felt like she'd stolen the air, while it was traveling to my lungs. As I sat in the dark triage room with the only light coming from the computer screens, my body wanted to collapse on the floor from humiliation. Her actions confirmed that I had not just imagined her as the

Big Bad Wolf—she'd been that way my whole life, always choosing torment in place of love.

Soon after Katrina sent me her first letter, others arrived printed on various types of copy paper. Some contained perforated holes at the top of the page, and others were a shade off from being bright white. She sent copies of several letters to five or six locations to ensure they would reach me. Each letter was typed in bold Arial font, or sometimes Georgia, as if she wanted more of an impact than the standard Times New Roman provided. Each letter was printed like a ransom note, missing a return address.

A couple months after Katrina's phone call, while working at the clinic's reception desk, I heard my name called on the overhead speakers: "Please come to Colonel Jones's office, please come to Colonel Jones's office." After scheduling a patient's follow-up appointment, I rushed down the hall.

The merlot-colored Berber carpet, which was speckled with bits of gray, gave clues that one was entering an area of importance. In contrast to the linoleum floors that were prevalent in-patient care areas such as Optometry, Gynecology, and Physical Therapy, it signified that I was in the leadership hall. Colonel Jones's office contained an elegant, U-shaped cherrywood executive desk with a hutch that had glass doors. The furnishings were a stark difference from the particleboard furniture in other offices. The light that peered through the blinds to the right of her desk assisted the fluorescent lighting in making the office look a little more welcoming.

Standing one beside the other in front of the commander's desk were five members of my chain of command. My supervisor, a black woman named Technical Sergeant Price, who had two daughters of her own, held cards and letters in one hand. She'd prayed for me many times while we worked together. Her faith in God, so strong and unapologetic, sometimes scared me. Her faith took center stage before any rank or military status, whereas my own faith remained shaky and inconsistent. I didn't know for sure if God was for or against me.

Technical Sergeant Price stood erect and faced the doorway, holding the letters high, clutched between her fingers. When she finally spoke, she said, "Your mother sent all of these to the Department of Defense, Air Combat Command, and to the base. She sent them to everybody she could, and they sent them to us. No one knows what to do with them. I've kept them away from you because I didn't want it to affect you at work." I didn't mention that I'd already received the same letters at home in addition to phone calls at both home and work.

In the letters, Katrina described me as a troubled child. She wrote about the time I lied about eating the Little Debbie snack. She attached printed information she'd found online related to schizophrenia. She begged the military to have me checked out by mental health professionals. She wrote about my failing grades in elementary school and the time I lied about breaking the salt shaker. She told them, "I've known since she was a child something wasn't right about her." Like in the other letters, she stoked the fire with a bit of personal info to show me she knew all about my life: "Good thing you live in an affordable apartment and drive an inexpensive car. Good choice. It's good on gas."

Glancing to my right, I saw that my commander, a black woman with a soft and intentional style of communicating, had a worried look on her face. I considered her too high in rank and too proper to relate to my situation. She reminded me of someone who used words like "gosh dang" and "sheesh" in place of real curse words. She maintained a natural face without makeup, and freckles of various sizes appeared underneath both eyes. She looked a little old fashioned; she wore her hair in a short, well-oiled bob with curls that sometimes looked as if they'd been formed by pink sponge rollers. I wondered if she came from an affluent, educated family. She reminded me of someone who graduated from an Ivy league school. Throughout my career, I would wonder how black women reached high ranks in the face of racism and misogyny. Did her smile mask the stress of her reality? I am sure she had overcome barriers, and I wished she could tell me her story. I often wondered if my career would follow a similar path. I looked up to her but never had the courage to tell her.

The three other women in the room were my first sergeant, superintendent, and deputy commander. They were white women whose contact with me was so minimal

I struggle to remember their names and physical features. After closing the door, one of them spoke to break the silence. "What's going on? We've never seen anything like this. Why would your own mother do this? She's your mother, right?" One of them said, "What's up with this lady? She sounds like a lunatic."

Glancing at each face, I searched for their real reactions. Did they genuinely care? Find it amusing? Or were they simply going through the motions? As a young staff sergeant, I couldn't be certain of anything—I didn't know them. As I stood before them, I wondered what they thought of me. I didn't know whether to spill the details of my childhood or pretend to be unmoved. I wanted to be simultaneously strong and weak. I worried about revealing any vulnerability for fear they would look at me differently. Years later when reminiscing about the meeting in the commander's office, I hoped I could be there for airmen and mentees in a respectful and empathetic way. Each woman gave me a snapshot of who I would one day become for young people in need of guidance and protection.

"Are you OK? Do you need anything from us? Do you feel safe? When is the last time you saw your mother? Do we need to make a call over to Legal to help you?"

All the words I wanted to say seemed to be locked between my tightly pursed lips. With my hands behind my back, I rubbed the skin on my fingers in anticipation of the rest of the conversation. My supervisor, sensing my uncomfortable vulnerability, asked us to pray. Four other women joined hands.

With eyes closed and head bowed, she said, "Father, we come to you today first saying thanks. Lord, you are a God who sees and knows all. God, we ask for your comfort and protection. Encamp your angels all around her ..."

As Technical Sergeant Price prayed, tears fell from our eyes. A knot formed in the middle of my chest, as I tried to contain the emotion. I felt gratitude for their support. Five women who were in charge of my career formed a circle with me and prayed for me. Before reading the letters, they'd only known me in a professional capacity. I'd never so much as uttered my mother's name to my coworkers. None of them said very much at the time or afterwards, but as we crossed paths, they looked at me differently. Weeks later, while walking down the hallway, Colonel Jones touched my shoulder and said, "I had no idea you went through all this. I am so sorry." Nodding my head, I said, "I know."

The letters continued to arrive at my home in droves, week after week. I called Momma, Maurice, Aunt Dorris, and everyone else I could think of to see if they could do something to make Katrina stop. No one offered much of anything in terms of advice, but they all acted shocked at the revelation of her actions. Instead, they offered platitudes: "Just ignore it. Pray for her."

Technical Sergeant Price, my supervisor, brought anointing oil to my office a few days after the meeting in the commander's office. She arrived to work early each morning to pray over the entire department. But on this day, she pleaded for God to protect me, as she placed the extra virgin olive oil around the doorframe of my office. She touched my desk, chair, computer, and keyboard, mouthing prayers at each turn. She said, "The devil is defeated. We are gonna anoint this evil spirit out of here."

A little while later, she stopped me, as I walked by her office. With her eyeglasses on the tip of her nose, she looked down at me and beckoned me to her office, as if I could read her mind or know instinctively what she would say next. She stood up, grabbed both of my hands, and held them as we prayed. I listened intently to each word, in disbelief that someone cared enough about me to stop me during the middle of the work day and pray. My face burned with the saltiness of my tears. Her prayers touched a part of me no one in the Air Force had witnessed. All the hurt my mother had caused was given to God right there at work. It reopened my channel to God and initiated a practice of prayer in my life which has sustained me through the darkest hours of my life.

She asked, "When is the last time you saw your mother?"

I said, "June 1997."

She replied, "Is she sick or on drugs?"

I said, "Ma'am, it all started with a letter I wrote to my mother asking forgiveness and letting her know I forgave her for past abuse. She's not on drugs, but she's got something mental going on."

My supervisor opened her filing cabinet and pulled out a folder. After each defamatory letter had arrived, she filed it in a blue file folder at the back of her filing cabinet. She said, "You don't have to worry about anyone else seeing these. They're going to stay right here, until you decide what you want to do with them."

My mother's disgusting, defamatory actions brought me into the presence of strong women who were real mothers and grandmothers. For once, I didn't have to handle the anger and shame alone. The women who prayed with me knew what it meant to protect the ones you love. They could not understand how a mother could cause harm to her own child.

Katrina's legacy is preserved in the letters she wrote, words she spoke, and messages she sent. It's also preserved in her actions—the way she treated me. She provided proof of how she felt about her only daughter. I have made peace with not having sweet memories of my mother. I have also made peace with not having a mother to rock me to sleep, nurse my bruised knees, or play Tooth Fairy.

When Momma reminisced about how Katrina behaved, she said, "She was always so fearful of everything. I don't know why she would do mean and hateful things for no reason." Now I understand.

CHAPTER 31

Hard Lessons

I wished for Katrina to be better, so I could be better. Together, we could have been better. Sometimes, forgiving others and being the bigger person doesn't produce the results we are looking for. Even if we do all the things people tell us we should do to make amends, the results can make our lives worse.

If I could tell my younger self anything, it would be to forgive Katrina in my own time and in my own way. I would say, "You don't need to make grand gestures to forgive your abusers. You don't need to prove to anyone that you have moved on and are accepting of the past. Life does not require you to keep in contact with people who poisoned you. You are allowed to move on without them. You are allowed to move far away, forget their phone numbers, and live as if they never existed. You don't need to explain the distance created by the painful memories they created. You have a right to be free. It's not your responsibility to try to patch up relationships with toxic people."

I'd also tell my younger self, "You are not required to change anything about who you are, so that your abusers will accept you. They don't want you to speak about the past, but it's your history—so speak up as often as you need to. It is OKAY for you to still weep from the memories of how they once stripped you of your dignity and self-worth. Cry as much as you need to and for as long as you need to. You don't have to forget your past in order to make life more comfortable for your abuser and those who were complicit in your suffering. The people who want you to move on only ask you to do so because of their own guilt, denial, and complacency. They don't want to face the reality of their part in your suffering. You remind them of the number of times they didn't call, didn't visit, and didn't remember you. You didn't matter then, and they don't and can't matter now. They don't get to dictate *how* and *when* you heal. You deserve to live in freedom, you deserve peace, and you deserve love. To the one who wanted nothing more than a family, I understand."

CHAPTER 32

Wanted

"Do not forget to show hospitality to strangers, for by so doing some people have shown hospitality to angels without knowing it."

~HEBREWS 13:2 (NIV)

The responsibilities of being a parent include the capacity to understand the weight of one's words. Children hang on to words spoken by the adults in their lives. When my mother told me I would be *nothing*, I believed her. I believed Katrina each time she told me I was *stupid* and said, "You'll never be anything in life. You're a failure." And when, under the guise of discipline, she beat me using belts, cords, boards, or fists, I believed I had no worth. Children remember words and silence alike. When my father and stepfather said nothing, they told me I didn't matter. Their silence equaled complicity in ongoing abuse. I imagine them as men who used both hands to cover their eyes, so they couldn't witness what they knew to be true.

Children also remember people by their proximity to everyday life. When children grow into adults, they never forget the way people made them feel. When I told family members about the physical and verbal abuse, they made a litany of excuses about Katrina's upbringing and told me to pray. I felt then and now that they were just as afraid of her as I was. I also believe they didn't care enough to endure the ripple effect that confrontation brings. But when we are hurt by others, we remember the people who welcomed us in and the ones who turned us away. Our memories guide and inform us later in life to remind us of who was safe and who was not. Children grow up blaming themselves for their suffering. Adults recollect childhood events and blame others.

I longed for my family members, who said they loved me, to hide me under their wings and protect me from the tumultuous storm of Katrina's rage. But they did nothing. As a child, I had favorite aunts and uncles; the ones who gave me nicknames, remembered my birthday, and always made me smile. I held on to their words, believing one day everything would be OKAY.

My family's toxicity and my mother's psychotic behavior didn't erase my desire to have a mother figure.

In fact, Katrina intensified my desire to have someone else fulfill that role. Each time I met an older woman, I thought, *I wish she could be my mother.* I longed to be adopted. I missed all the things I'd never had, like Mom hugs, being cared for when I was ill, phone calls, and having someone to listen and give advice. I longed for someone older and wiser to make a long-term investment in me. I looked forward to the day when I could be a mom and a mentor for other young women.

I wore an invisible sign upon my chest: WANTED: Mothers who don't hurt, don't hit, and don't have rage buried within the depths of their bones. Mothers who know how to give life lessons without harming their children in the process. Mothers who will hold me and have healing in the palms of their hands. Mothers who use their voices to encourage, uplift, and inspire me to be my best self. Mothers to show me what it means to be a woman. I need a mother's lap, shoulder, arms, smile, eyes, ears, and lips.

Knowing this, God sent angels in the form of women. One angel was an eighty-year-old white woman who shared her home with her daughter and four-year-old granddaughter. They lived next door to me when I was about nine years old and lived in Gravel Ridge, AR, just outside of the Air Force base.

Ms. Cook stood about five feet tall and wore tightly wound curls in her dyed-brown hair. About once or twice per month, she baked my family a moist, delicious cake that included tart Granny Smith apples, brown sugar, and chopped pecans. After school, I would run directly to her house, eagerly knocking on her door and hoping she'd made a sweet treat that day. She always opened the door wearing button-down, pink shirts with matching pants. Her home contained a menagerie of crystal decorations, Precious Moments figurines, and family pictures that cluttered the end tables. The living room and kitchen were a far cry from Momma's house. Ms. Cook's home always smelled like freshly washed linen, and the kitchen floors were so shiny I could almost see my reflection in the linoleum. As she prepared dinner for her family, I either stood next to her or sat at the oval, claw-foot table. As she cooked, she watched *Wheel of Fortune* or *Jeopardy*. I gravitated to her out of longing for my own grandmother.

Another angel came to me during high school—this one attended my church. Until I met Pam, I didn't know role models existed. We met when she opened the door to the small room my friends and I sat in while we chuckled and held side conversations during Vacation Bible School. As she cracked open the door, my friends and I snapped our heads in her direction. I immediately noticed the way her cheeks rose upward when she smiled and how her skin was so smooth and unblemished. Her skin, as dark chocolate-colored as my own, proved beauty could be found in all complexions. She looked as if God had dipped her into Hershey's milk chocolate, and I wanted to know everything about her, so that I could be like her. I wanted to wear red lipstick and long, flowy dresses with pointy heels just like her. Her captivatingly beautiful brown eyes told me I could trust her. I'd never met anyone with such grace, sophistication, and kindness. She was the kind of woman whose voice danced with a certain cadence between both cheeks and onto the tip of her tongue before reaching your ears. I didn't know her age at the time, but she seemed to be in her late thirties or early forties. She had the bone structure and unblemished skin of a woman about whom people often remarked, "You look so young for your age."

When my friends and I stood in the church foyer each day, I impatiently surveyed the parking lot waiting for Pam's arrival. I watched her walk toward the entryway and looked forward to any form of acknowledgment she might offer. The way she wrapped her arms around me in a tight embrace—sometimes even holding the back of my head—made me feel like I was her daughter. As she spoke, she sometimes touched my arm with her hand to add emphasis, making me feel seen. She had a natural way of being warm and compassionate to each person she greeted.

Outside of church, we spoke on the phone anytime Katrina was away from home. As I vented to Pam about my life, living in fear of Katrina, she often responded with, "I don't know what to do. If I report her, I don't know where you'll go. If I speak to her, something bad could happen to you." She told me, "The devil will have to move out of the way. Every day, I want you to read Psalms 91. Memorize it and add your name to the scripture."

During later phone calls, she would ask with urgency in her voice, "Are you reading your Bible? Don't stop. God is moving. He has to respond." Pam cried with me, urging me to keep going and not give up on my purpose in life. I loved Pam as much as I loved Momma—so much that there are no words or comparisons to depict how I felt about her. She wasn't just nice to me—she was also a dedicated listener who took time to seriously consider everything I shared with her.

When we ended our calls, I was always spiritually full. She was able to ignite and fan the flames of whatever hope resided within me during my darkest moments. I considered us a team, working together to cast out evil spirits as I read the Bible ferociously. In a lot of ways, I saw Pam as my mother, sister, auntie, and friend. I trusted her more than I trusted any other adult in my life, and I trusted what she said about God. I believed in her prayers and her interpretation of scripture. When I read the scripture, I did so with authority, just like Pam had taught me to do. I felt like I was on assignment, as if the reading would tear down walls, mountains, anything that prevented me from being safe. Talking to God helped me to feel like there were angels working in heavenly realms to keep Katrina from harming me. I knew that even if Katrina beat me, she could not kill the spirit God had placed inside of me. Before I met Pam, I didn't know scriptures could be applied to my life and used to summon God's response. Years later, we lost contact as she got married, soon to be divorced, and then happily remarried. She turned down my offers to visit and invitations to celebrate important milestones in my life. I interpreted her "no" responses personally, and saw them as signs she no longer wanted to be a part of my life. I would rethink every conversation, every decision, and every choice I'd made to place her on such a high pedestal.

Although various women helped to mentor and counsel me during each season of my life, it didn't take away the longing for biological connections with my family in Arkansas. I wanted family members who watched me grow. Every person I met, including Pam, had a family of their own. During my first four years in the Air Force, I thought a lot about Momma and what it would be like to repay her for taking care of me and loving me when I needed her most. What if she could move in with me? I could take her out of her dilapidated old house and use my modest income to help her pay off medical bills.

I spoke with the Air Force representatives in charge of military health insurance and benefits to find out what I would need to do to make her a military dependent. I fantasized about what my life would look like having Momma stay with me in my two-bedroom apartment. I knew it would be a long shot, but at least I could dream. I made mental notes, weighing the pros against the cons. Pros: for the first time in my life, I could introduce my coworkers and church friends to a member of my family. I wouldn't come home and have just the television and computer to keep me company—I'd have someone to share the details of my day with. I could show her how much I appreciated her. At the same time, there were many cons: Momma would be removed from her home, children, and grandchildren. She wouldn't know anyone but me in Idaho. While I worked all day, she wouldn't have anyone to keep her company. She'd miss the familiarity of her everyday life. The winters in Idaho wouldn't be kind to her fragile frame. My apartment was upstairs, and it would not be easy for her to climb a dozen wooden stairs before she even reached the front door. Also, what would happen when I deployed or changed duty stations? Lastly, Momma had twelve real, biological children. Most had homes and were doing well financially. She didn't live with them, so why should I believe she would move to be with me? I knew my desires for Momma to live with me were born from my well of loneliness. I also knew my desires were selfish. How dare I want her all to myself?

I called her and pitched her the idea, "Don't you want to move in with me?"

"Girl, what am I going to do there? My life is here." Her response was decisive and swift.

I paused at the question, hoping it wasn't rhetorical. "But if you move in with me, I can take care of you, and I'll pay all your bills. You won't ever have to clean, cook, or do anything you don't want to do."

She responded, "I can't move 'cause I won't be needed. I got to have something to do during the day, and my grandchildren need me."

She'd once been my whole world, and I wanted a slice of that world back. I deserved to have my whole world returned to me. Even though I understood her reasons, her response felt like rejection, and I felt another door I desperately wanted to keep open slamming shut. I took the rejection very hard and felt crushed by the lack of familial love and support in my day-to-day life. My life didn't matter to my family. My life didn't matter to anyone. Why should my life matter to me? A very dark cloud started to descend over me, and the black fog of depression began to be my only companion.

CHAPTER 33

What's Love?

Kelvin and I met in our early twenties while living in the dorms at Mountain Home Air Force Base. All unmarried airmen who did not have children were mandated to live in the dorms until they were married, with child, or had served in the military for at least two-and-a-half or three years. He lived on the third floor, and I lived on the first. He passed my room often when he was on the way to visit his friends. Eventually, Kelvin and I hung in the same circle of friends. He stood six feet tall, weighed 160 pounds, and had a thick Alabama twang. He made me feel less insecure about my Arkansas accent. When people heard me talk, they would laughingly remark, "You're country. Where are you from?"

I'll never forget the way Kelvin looked at me with his shifty brown eyes through his thick, brown, government-issued bifocals. His eyes burst forward, as if they were being viewed through the lens of a magnifying glass. As he spoke, he often bit his fingernails while looking to the left or right at nothing in particular. He gave the impression of being shy, but later I discovered him to be far, far from the timid, inexperienced impression he created. Either way, he pushed me out of my own timidity. As we talked, I figured one of us would have to learn how to look the other in the eye, so we could get to know each other.

We started talking more while hanging out in the dorm's day room, a recreational area with big-screen televisions, seating, and pool tables. It's the spot where my dorm-mates and I listened to Mystikal and Busta Rhymes while chugging strawberry-flavored Arbor Mist and Boones Farm. When Kelvin first began flirting, he did so by stopping me in the hall on his way to finishing laundry. Each conversation began with, "Uh, what you doing today?" I appreciated the effort, and courage he showed in approaching me. Other times, he asked friends about my relationship status. I didn't take him seriously, thinking him to be too nerdy and awkward for my taste. I also wondered if our mutual acquaintances were encouraging his advances, or if I was a dare of some sort among boys who thought of themselves as players.

I told him, "If you're serious, come to church." The following Sunday, he proved himself by coming to our small storefront church dressed to impress with black

trousers, a white button-down dress shirt, and a silver tie.
I giggled as I turned and saw him sitting in the back row
of chairs with a few of our mutual friends. Afterwards,
he said, "Well, I came to church. Will you talk to me
now?" I was still only mildly interested in him, but I felt
flattered by his advances. I liked Kelvin because he kept
his Nikes store-bought white and lined against the wall,
without creases that showed wear. He wore white tanks
underneath short-sleeved Polo shirts in various colors
that never faded. His skin also maintained a cocoa butter
shine even in the dead of winter. And when he laughed, he
laughed with his head held back, face toward the ceiling.
When he laughed, he made me laugh, too.

Our backgrounds were eerily similar. We were both
raised in the Deep South, and his family history also
included sexual abuse, harsh discipline, and a strict religious upbringing. When he talked about his stepfather's
abuse, he did so to empathize with me. He trusted me
with a past he had not shared with anyone else. Both of us
had complicated relationships and family secrets too full
of tumult to speak about openly. During deployments and
other military-related travel, we maintained a long-distance relationship. He emailed long letters in which he
promised to be good, faithful, and careful with my heart.
The silly schoolgirl in me clung to his promises. The more
mature part of me thought, *Be careful.* Part of me wanted
to stay single long enough to find myself, but the other
part of me needed to be with someone who made me feel
like I mattered.

When we were together, we spent our weekends playing raucous games like Pictionary and Spades or drinking tequila with dorm friends. He loved guns, and on one of our first dates, he took me to a local armory and taught me how to shoot. We were the only black people there. The bearded, stringy-haired white man behind the counter smirked each time Kelvin requested to hold a weapon, but Kelvin didn't care about the onlookers and all-white staff. Men in camouflaged jackets watched him as he reveled and asked to hold various weapons. Outside of the military-issued M-16, I had no experience with or interest in weapons.

Katrina had often bragged about the .22 caliber handgun she kept in her glove compartment and sometimes in her purse, and I had sometimes wondered if she would ever use it to kill me or her husband. The memory stoked my fear of guns and people who purchased guns for hobbies like hunting and recreational shooting. Although I feared guns and found them unnecessary, Kelvin taught me the proper way to hold and shoot.

Our friends laughed at our relationship because of his quiet country personality and my straightforward communication style. During our three-year relationship, there were rumors about his sexual proclivities because other females on base gossiped about sleeping with him. But I ignored the warnings from my close friends. I pushed away the alarms that told me to break up with him, even after I realized we weren't a good fit for each other. When we were together, he treated me nicely and, most of all, he told me he loved me. I wanted to believe him and told him the same.

He often brought up marriage. I encouraged his pursuit by going to the mall with a close friend to try on engagement rings. I cared for Kelvin as much as I could, but I didn't feel that kind of love for him. My fear of being alone, and the deep desire to prove to myself that I could love and be loved kept our relationship going. One day, he asked if I would like to go eat ice cream at a little mom-and-pop shop known for its oversized portions. I remember feeling so special and giddy at someone asking me to do to something as simple as go out for ice cream. Moments like that cemented my decision to stay in the relationship. I thought, *What if no one else comes along to ask me on a date?*

In the third year of our relationship, one evening after we were both home from work, he knocked on my dorm room door , interrupting my nap. I loved the way he waited for me to answer before walking into my unlocked room. My body faced away from him and towards the wall as he sat on the edge of the bed and said, "Turn over and look at me. I love you. I've been wanting to marry you for a long time. Will you marry me?" He then revealed a black velvet jewelry box. Inside was a one-carat, princess-cut diamond ring. It was the same ring I had tried on weeks before with my friend. Smiling sheepishly, I said, "Yes," and we embraced. A few weeks later, nervous and unsure about my decision, my voice shook, as I sat on his lap to hug him and said, "Please don't hurt me. You know my past."

He held me tight. "I would never do anything to hurt you."

I rationalized my decision to marry by thinking, *If it doesn't work out, we can always get a divorce.* At about twenty-one years of age, I figured I had time to change my mind if the relationship or marriage didn't work out. If my past had taught me anything, it was that the people who say they love you *will* hurt you. For reasons I can't explain, I felt like I wouldn't have time to meet anyone new if I didn't marry Kelvin. I couldn't see past the present. I thought, *What if Kelvin is the only person who will ever love me? What if I never get another chance to experience marriage?*

We had sex only once during our three-year courtship. I told myself I would remain celibate until after marriage. I made this decision a few months before meeting Kelvin. I wanted my body to feel pure again. I felt conflicted about what day I had lost my virginity. Did I lose it the day my brother touched me, or did it happen when I gave my body to Reggie? Either way, it had been too long since my body knew the feeling of being untouched. After having more sexual partners than I could count, my body felt heavy, as if it held the DNA of each person I'd slept with. I imagined that if my vagina could have spoken, it would have said, "Enough. Road Closed. Danger. Do not enter." Even as my mind forgot the names of each partner, my mind remained convinced that my sexual encounters had stamped my body with a toxic waste of some sort. I wanted to feel clean, pure, and healthy again.

During the one-time encounter with Kelvin, I began to cry. He asked, "What's wrong? Does it hurt?" The sex didn't seem worth the sacrifice. I had given up my vow of celibacy to satisfy his sexual urges. I did so amid rumors of him cheating and felt wholly responsible for his infidelity. Our mutual guy friends told me, "If he's not getting it from you, he's going to get it from someone." Who in their right mind would expect a man to be faithful for three years without having sex? After the experience, I hated myself for giving in to something that in no way gave me pleasure or assured me that he would be faithful.

When we spoke to our church's pastor and first lady about our desire to have a small wedding at the church, the pastor voiced ambivalence about our readiness to be married. He cited our age, maturity levels, and sporadic church attendance. He warned us that if premarital counseling didn't go well, he wouldn't marry us. For eight weeks, we met with the pastor and lied about our relationship, the depths of our faith, and our finances. We lied when we told the pastor we were prepared for the challenges of being married. After leaving the counseling sessions, we laughed off the pastor's concerns and labeled him as nosy and judgmental. The pastor, seeing through our ignorance, begged us to wait. In a matter-of-fact tone, he said, "Neither of you is ready for marriage."

A few months later, we were scheduled to wed at the church in a private ceremony in front of a few coworkers and friends. *I let the relationship go too far, for too long,* I thought as we drove to the church. Sitting in the passenger side of Kelvin's white Chevrolet Cavalier, I noticed the television remote on my lap. In our haste to get to the church on time, I had grabbed the remote instead of my wallet. *Why am I doing this?* A close male acquaintance had tried to tell me to cut the relationship off well before we were even engaged. He had witnessed Kelvin cheating and, unbeknownst to me, had also heard rumors of at least five or six girls who had slept with Kelvin during our relationship.

Just prior to the wedding ceremony, once again I had feelings of strong reservation, and I told myself, *I should just cancel it.* But people were there, standing as we entered the church's sanctuary. Someone had decorated it with flowers and gotten me a bouquet of white roses. I thought about Kelvin and how embarrassing it would be for him if I stopped the wedding. I pushed aside the gossip and rumors to save both of us from shame.

I wore a shimmery cream sheath dress with a matching cropped short-sleeve jacket. I have no recollection of what Kelvin wore, but I remember him being excited, smiling from ear to ear. I kept our wedding a secret. He told his coworkers and our group of friends, but I felt ashamed by my decision to marry the first guy who told me he loved me. I was also embarrassed by not having anyone in my family present on such an important day.

I didn't have a father to walk me down the aisle, and I was acutely aware of the absence of a parent figure on this major occasion—I longed for the love of my real father, and I wondered if he was out there somewhere thinking of me, wondering what his child looked like now that she was all grown up and getting married. I imagined him smiling, as he gave me away to Kelvin and thought about how proud I would have felt to have him there. But on our supposedly special day, I didn't even have bridesmaids to laugh with, cry with, pray with, party with ...

The ceremony ended quickly, and we didn't have a reception. His friends and coworkers returned to work. We returned to the dorms, and all I could think was, *Is this the part where we have to have sex?*

Within a week or two, we moved out of the dorms and into a one-bedroom, one-bath upstairs duplex that was owned by the elderly couple next door. The apartment reminded me of something from the seventies with its brown shag carpet, speckled yellow Formica countertops, and wood-paneled walls. When it rained, the popcorn-textured ceiling leaked. I purchased all the furniture and paid our monthly bills. When I looked around at our shared space, I felt proud of myself for being able to afford everything we needed and for having my own car. I had done everything on my own with no help from friends or family.

Again, I longed for the presence of an absent father. I wished my biological father could see the little place, help me hang photos on the wall, remind me to get my vehicle's oil changed, and give his opinion about Kelvin. Still, I tried my best to make it work—alone. On weekends I prepared homemade banana pudding, collard greens, fried chicken, and cornbread. I became addicted to purchasing Pampered Chef kitchen utensils and bakeware. On weekdays, I baked cakes, pasta salad, and homemade pizzas for my coworkers.

Kelvin and I were uncomfortable in our roles as husband and wife. Being married felt like a daily chore and too much responsibility. We arrived home from work bored with one another and tired of repetitive conversations about our jobs and what to eat for dinner. I coped with my feelings by eating until I was half-past full. Within a few months, my bras burst from my newly developed double-D breasts. Always one to wear loose-fitting clothes, I didn't notice the added thirty pounds, until I saw photos revealing swollen cheeks. I was sitting on Kelvin's lap one day when he said, "Get off me. You're too heavy." He spent most of his time outside of work with friends. I spent my time alone or with friends from church—endlessly venting about our relationship. Kelvin and I argued more than we kissed, held hands, or laughed. Between the struggles of being an adult, being newly married, and not having a support system, life became overwhelming.

Most of the airmen we worked with were in relationships and married quickly, partially because it gave them permission to move out of the dorms and off base. Living off base made us all feel a little more independent and adult. I assumed our shared group of friends would eventually come around to our apartment and hang out. But they didn't. Instead, Kelvin and I became more removed from the social circle of mutual friends we once shared, and we got lost in our own lives, problems, and goals. We found new ways to numb ourselves. I numbed the truth about my loneliness by refusing to speak up about the fragility of my emotions. I didn't tell anyone that being physically by myself for extended periods felt like being deserted, orphaned, and forgotten. I hadn't acknowledged to myself the ways in which I was already vulnerable due to my upbringing, when I had been restricted from having platonic relationships. When the phone stopped ringing and the invites stopped coming, I assumed no one cared.

Cue TLC's song "What About Your Friends."

CHAPTER 34

Fragility

This marriage is over. I can't keep living like this, I thought.

Kelvin coped with the stress and disappointment of marriage by staying away from our apartment. I didn't have the energy to chase him or play detective. One attempt to follow him quickly failed because I feared he would see my car. If I couldn't be a good detective and complete my mission unnoticed, I didn't want to investigate at all. I returned to our apartment and overthought myself to sleep. Emotionally, I began to spiral downward and was resigned to the fact that I had ruined my one good chance at love.

Our union imploded before it even had a chance to pick up steam. With only my mind to keep me occupied, I created the belief that told me no one wanted me in their lives and no one would care if I died. Loneliness forced me to confront the validity of my relationships, but not until after I got married. Over and over again, I asked myself, *Does my husband really care about me? Are my friends really my friends? When they say they love me, are they telling the truth? If my life really matters, why am I all alone?* Because of my loneliness, I no longer trusted or believed in myself. When I allowed my mind to run rampant, it felt almost like I was on the edge of a psychotic break—one in which a return to wellness or normality wouldn't be guaranteed.

Loneliness dominated my life in such a permanent state that no other alternate feelings which might have given me relief from my constant sense of loneliness stood a chance. I forgot about the strides I'd made to free myself from Katrina. The fact that I'd graduated high school, joined the Air Force, and had relationships did not seem like wins. It all seemed unearned and too ordinary. In those moments of fragility, it was difficult to find reasons to live. Like my expectation that the military would allow me to feel like I belonged to a family, I wholly and deeply craved for my friends to embody my idea of the perfect family. In my mind, my friends were supposed to be there no matter what changes occurred in their own lives. As people got married, pregnant, and busy with attaining rank, my invites to be a part of their lives were somehow misplaced. They moved on without me and did not seem to miss my presence. I felt as if I'd been thrown away like old furniture at a landfill.

Kelvin's proclivities to sleep around and hang with his friends triggered memories of Katrina's words about no man ever wanting me. I reinforced her claims by telling myself no one wanted me. That one thought grew as fast as a gasoline-lit forest fire, damaging everything in its path. I'd gotten myself into the situation of marrying too soon and for the wrong reasons, and I didn't see an easy way out. I didn't know how I would survive being alone. I looked at his collection of guns: a 9 mm revolver, a .45 caliber pistol, and a .22 caliber handgun. A couple of times, I held each one in my hands and thought, *What if I kill myself?* The lonely nights with nothing but my thoughts caused insomnia, so I sometimes took more Benadryl than I needed to help me sleep. Sometimes, I took five or six Vicodin. When I'd wake up, I would continue with life as if everything was—okay. I did this to cope with overwhelming emotions I baked desserts like banana pudding, Ms. Cook's apple nut cake, and pound cake—then ate myself sick. I exercised only when I needed to maintain some level of military fitness.

My faith in God faltered—I attended church but didn't feel like I measured up to God's expectations. At work, I pretended to be OKAY. When people asked about married life, I told them what I thought they wanted to hear. On the outside, I looked like I had a stable life. I had left an abusive home, begun a career, gotten married, and joined a church. On the inside, I felt robbed by God and hated everything about myself. I'd grown from being a lonely, awkward child restricted from having close relationships, to a woman with so much emotional baggage, I felt clueless about how to foster relationships with anyone. I asked God over and over why I couldn't have what came effortlessly for others. I wondered why I had to be so alone and why no one could be there for me. I began praying for God to take my life just like I had as a child. I also asked God why I couldn't fit in with anyone. I pleaded with God for answers but didn't get any responses.

I felt as if I was caught in a torrential downpour—the depression stayed with me not one, two, or three days per week but five or six. Even while I concentrated on other facets of life, such as my job, self-destructive thoughts loomed around the corner. Every conversation I had, had the potential to trigger a downward depressive spiral. The depression came as I stood in front of my stove frying pork chops with gravy, sweet potato yams, and sautéed green beans. Each time I created a meal, I wished Momma and the family I loved so deeply in Arkansas could share it with me. The depression came in the mornings, as I showered and sang my favorite songs. The music reminded me how much I had loved music when I was growing up. The depression came in the spring and summer when most people cheered up. For me, however, those times signaled that I would not have anyone to vacation with, and no one would be taking a vacation to visit me. The depression surfaced in both expected and unexpected moments, and it was always there.

* * *

About six months into my marriage, I'd had enough. On a cold, misty February morning, as Kelvin slept, I laid in bed next to him, pleading for God to give me permission to end the marriage. Impatient for God's reply, I leaped out of bed as if I were late for work. I plopped down in our desk chair in the corner of the living room. I smirked when I saw Kelvin was still logged in on AOL. An instant message alert popped up on the screen: "Hello, wyd?" Pretending to be him, I responded, "Nothing." I hoped the person would reply with small details indicating the nature of their relationship. But this didn't happen, and I couldn't imitate him since I didn't know anything about their typical conversations. Giving up my idea to impersonate him online, I ended the conversation with a simple "See you later."

Noticing his black backpack on the floor, I opened it. There were cards and photos hidden between loosely nestled papers. In the photos, a female with a caramel complexion and bobbed, curly hair wore a purple satin, lace-trimmed negligée. Next to her, stood a smiling woman who wore a matching black bra and panty set. Both women were around twenty or twenty-one years old. They looked like they'd either made love to each other or were about to have a threesome. They appeared to be sexy, mischievous, and fueled by Jose Cuervo. I didn't have to wonder if that's where my husband spent work nights and weekends. In another lifetime, I might have wanted to spend my time with them as well. Scattered among the pictures were hot pink and red greeting cards, one given to him on Valentine's Day. The unknown sender said she loved him and begged him to leave me. She was married with an infant who was only a few months old, but she pledged to leave her husband as well. As I read the card, I thought back to Valentine's Day. He had arrived home that night around 8:00 p.m. with flowers and an unsigned card. I'd waited all day for him to come home. I had wondered how we would spend the day. That night, I'd sat on the couch facing the front door and waiting for him to appear. How foolish I felt being married and alone on the one day made for couples to celebrate love.

After snooping, I screamed for Kelvin to wake up. We argued as I threw pillows, phones, and anything else within my reach. As if I were in a scene from a dramatic comedy, I stood near the kitchen counter while hurling newly purchased dinner plates at his face. I raged, feeling duped because he'd convinced me to give him a chance. Although we weren't in love, marriage had signified a chance for me to grow to love someone—to grow and find my own form of happiness. Marriage had meant never being alone again. Marriage had meant I belonged to someone. I had assumed we would grow to love one another, and he would fill the parts of me that had been left barren by my own family. I hadn't yet come to the realization that we'd lied to one another. We were both too young and too emotionally damaged for marriage. As we continued to argue, he admitted to the affair and said, "She ain't nothing but a hoe."

CHAPTER 35

I Don't Wanna Die, But…

During the courtship and marriage to Kelvin, I had a new and trustworthy confidant in Stephanie, a friend who I met through my church community. We grew to become sisters to each other. When I first met her, I discovered Stephanie's voice had the full-bodied deepness of a soulful black woman, although she was white. She was about ten years my senior, married, and a mother of one at the time; later, she would have six more children. We met at our nondenominational, racially diverse church, and I was hungry to meet *good* and God-fearing people. It was the same church where Kelvin and I wed. She and her husband Harold, a black Air Force member, had met during her college days in Boise. I looked up to them because of their conservative Christian family values. She set an example for myself and other young women on how to be a godly wife.

Stephanie had everything I also hoped to have one day: a successful marriage, stable home, close friends, and happy children. She talked to me about the difficulties of marriage. Her husband was a minister, and he talked a lot about God. Within minutes of him arriving home, I'd often see him studying his Bible. Stephanie, a stay-at-home mom, made married life look attainable. I reveled at the way she catered to her family's needs. She'd come from a large, loving, connected family. She knew what it meant to feel loved, and oozed the very definition of it through her pores. She had been with me the day I tried on engagement rings and again the day Kelvin and I wed. She listened, prayed, and stood by me more than anyone else had throughout my adult life.

Kelvin left after we argued about his affair, and I called Stephanie immediately. Through loud, forceful tears, I shared with her my feelings of being tired of being unloved. I wept, wailed, and kept repeating, "I'm so tired. I'm so tired." Stephanie listened as intently as Pam had in my youth, and she quieted me by asking to pray for me. We stayed on the phone for about an hour, during which I couldn't help but think of what I might do if she ever said, "Can I call you back later?" As she prayed and pleaded to God on my behalf, I knew she could read between the lines of my words. I wanted to end my suffering. I didn't want to die, but I would if it meant I didn't have to feel the way I felt ever again. I didn't want to die; I just wanted to feel like I belonged to someone. While she prayed, I felt guilty for taking time away from her family.

How could she understand my pain, when she had a close-knit family and parents who loved her? While she prayed, I convinced myself of what a terrible decision it had been to call her in the first place. Why would I burden my friend? She would surely change her good opinion of me after seeing me in such a deeply vulnerable place. And what if Harold blamed me for being in this position? I cared about what he and others thought of me. What if my life of sin had placed me in my current predicament? Who in our church would even understand when everyone I encountered seemed so happy and free each Sunday? Everyone else floated, while I trudged along.

The affair hurt more than it otherwise would have because Kelvin had begged me to marry him. He'd said all the right things, and a part of me wanted to believe him. I felt used for giving my body to someone who didn't deserve it. I felt used for the money I'd spent to create our home. I blamed Kelvin by thinking, *Why would he cheat on me, when he knows I don't have anyone else?*

After hanging up the phone with Stephanie, Kelvin appeared in the entryway of our bedroom, his words were inaudible, as he begged for forgiveness. My thoughts were louder than his apology. The voice in my mind repeated, *You're worthless. You can't even find one person to love you. You should give up.* At twenty-one years old, I made up my mind that I'd given my life long enough to get better. As an expert on my own pain, it was hard for me to imagine a different reality. I chalked up my time using earth's resources as wasted time. Kelvin left my site briefly. I stood up from the bed, walked to the closet, and stood on the tips of my toes to grab hold of Kelvin's .45 caliber handgun. The voices said over and over, *You don't have any family. You don't have anyone. No one is going to miss you. No one cares.* I had no evidence to the contrary. Kelvin returned to the bedroom and found me sitting on the edge of our bed, as I held the gun in my right hand.

Frantic, he said, "What are you doing? Don't do that!" He was helpless and afraid to come close to me.

I said, "I'm so tired of everyone in my life hurting me." Aiming the gun at the left side of my chest, near my heart, I pulled the trigger.

Kelvin placed both of his hands on his forehead and screamed, "No, no, no! Why did you do that?" He grabbed the gun and dialed 911. While he waited on the operator to answer the call, he grabbed my arm and guided me to the door.

As he gave the details and address to the operator, I yelled, "This is your fault!" I wanted the 911 operator to hear me blame him. I wanted him to suffer for pushing me to insanity. As he spoke to the operator, I sat against the wall, on the old linoleum floor, directly in front of the door that led outside. The daylight burst through the screen door as if to awaken me. In that moment, I didn't feel any pain. The evidence of what I'd done existed only on my white button-down shirt. Blood stained the area near the wound and dripped down my side and onto my pants. I thought about what my neighbors might think of me. Would they call me crazy? What about my coworkers and church members?

Suicide meant putting an end to being let down. The first person to let me down had been my mother, who had abused and neglected my needs. The man I called my father had chosen his other family over me. My brother sexually abused me. The few friends I'd made in the military were nowhere to be found. I had grown tired of being the least important person in everyone's life. Major achievements and milestone birthdays always passed with no one there. I'd played Russian roulette with my life by shooting myself in an area near my heart. I didn't want to die, but I wanted God to save me from the pain. I wanted freedom from pretending.

As I waited on the ambulance, I could see eight-foot crape myrtle trees through a window. The weather outside betrayed the dark cloud that existed in our apartment. My conscience spoke, and a voice that sounded like my own said, "Your life isn't over. You are not going to die. It's not your time. You have more work to do." It felt like the voice of God encouraging me. After examining me at the hospital, the emergency physician, a man with short gray hair and a stern face, remarked, "I don't know how you're still alive. The bullet you used is designed to mushroom. It should have hit all of your internal organs, but it got stuck in your side and stopped near your waist." At the hospital, Stephanie and her husband stood next to my gurney.

I stayed in the hospital's psychiatric unit for three days.

A petite nurse with bobbed blonde hair visited me daily. She said she had to observe me, and I couldn't be left alone. After she checked my pulse, she sat in the chair next to my bed and asked if she could pray with me. Standing up, she looked at me as said, "God isn't finished with you. Promise me you won't ever try to end your life again." I looked into her eyes and promised.

Kelvin came to see me later that night. Holding back tears, he apologized again for cheating. I could see the sincerity in his facial expressions. I, too, apologized for blaming him for my actions and for the hours law enforcement had spent questioning him. During my stay, the psychologist interviewed me and determined that I could return to work and my life. He said, "Everyone gets depressed in life. I don't think anything is wrong with you, and I see no reason to recommend further treatment. We will all experience at least three depressive episodes in our lifetime." After I was released from the hospital, I decided it would be best to end the marriage.   Years later, Kelvin would find me on Facebook. He repeated his regrets about our relationship failures and said he wished things had been different. We were young and both too broken for marriage. In our last conversation, Kelvin shared about his new marriage, career, children, and strong, devout faith in God. He said, "I go to church now, and if I'd had God in my life at the time, I wouldn't have cheated." Suicide almost robbed me of my future. But if my thoughts could lead to hopelessness, why couldn't they also lead to hope?

CHAPTER 36

That One Friend

One of my first friendships, which lasted only a couple of months and occurred while I lived with Katrina, may have been the first sign of my attraction to the same sex. Katrina introduced me to Danielle, a chubby girl with dark eyes and a mischievous smile, by saying she was new in the neighborhood. Danielle was the kind of girl boys made fun of because of her body frame and short, pigtailed hair. She lived six doors down from us in a brown house with tan shutters. It felt far away to me because I was rarely allowed to walk or ride my bike down the street.

Lavonne said to Katrina, "We moved into the neighborhood last month, and Danielle needs a good friend." I didn't want to get my hopes up, but I thought I needed

a friend, too. I looked forward to us watching *Rugrats* together. At nine years old, Danielle was only a year younger
than I was. She lived with her mother and sixteen-year-
old brother. But, unlike me, she looked up to her brother,
who worked at Pizza Hut. Danielle described him as the
man of the house, protective of her and their mother. She
said, "Brent makes sure no one messes with me."

Danielle stopped by the house one day with her mother, and announced, "You're my new friend." *She's weird*,
I thought, as I smiled and introduced myself. Katrina
and Danielle's mother stood outside and talked for a bit,
while Danielle and I sized each other up. I spent the rest
of that day and the following days fantasizing about the
possibility of having a new friend. I wondered, *What does
her house look like? What does her mom act like? How did her
mom meet Katrina?* But more to the point, *Does Danielle's
mom act anything like Katrina?* It turned out that Lavonne,
a dark-skinned woman with a short pixie cut and bags
under her eyes, worked two jobs. Like Katrina, she was a
heavy cigarette smoker.

A few weeks later, she knocked on the door and asked
if I could go trick-or-treating with her. Katrina gave permission and looked in the closet to see what kind of costume
we could create. Finding an old pair of denim overalls, a
plaid shirt, and a straw hat, we created a costume kind of
resembling a clown, scarecrow, or farmer. Katrina used
her make-up to draw squiggly lines on my face along with
black lips and darkened, exaggerated eyes. With plastic
bags in hand, Danielle and I raced from house to house.

Katrina followed closely behind in her car.

A few days later, Danielle rang the doorbell after school. "Wanna come to my house?"

Before I could ask, Katrina yelled, "Go ahead!"

When we got there, Danielle said, "My mom and brother are at work, but they'll be home soon. We can sit on the floor if you want."

We settled on the shaggy, olive green living room carpet. She lay on her back, as if she were preparing for an examination. I lay on my side, alternating between watching her and taking in the details of her home.

Letting out a nervous giggle, I said, "She don't let me play with anyone."

Danielle said, "You wanna play Mommy and Daddy?'

"Yeah," I replied.

We began by rubbing each other's arms, using our fingertips to explore our bellies. I thought, *What if her brother comes home early and sees us?* I listened for the sound of cars or voices outside.

Prior to this moment of exploration, I hadn't had a conscious thought regarding my attraction to males or females. I'd liked little boys since the age of four, the first being a biracial kid with thick, curly locks. But on that day with Danielle, I liked her in the same way I liked little boys. When most kids play doctor, it's usually out of curiosity, and it's normal to want to see if other little boys and girls have what you have. But the experience with Danielle felt different because my body had already been touched in all the wrong ways. I recognized the differences between her touch, and how I felt when my own brother abused me. The comfort and safety I felt with Danielle made me want to return to that feeling later in life.

CHAPTER 37

Who's In, Who's Outed?

After the marriage ended, my loneliness led me to pursue online relationships. I entertained myself by joining AOL, AIM, and Yahoo chatrooms. Hours would go by without me taking time to eat, bathe, or brush my teeth. From sunup to sundown, I engaged in conversations with anonymous women online. They all began the same way: age, sex, location or "A/S/L?" The anonymity, spontaneity, and taboo topic of raunchy sexual fantasies excited me. Online, I could pretend to be a bold, adventurous yoni master. There was something particularly naughty about sitting in my living room wearing oversized pajamas while chatting with people about my sexual interests on my Dell laptop.

I spent entire weekends occupying the left-side couch cushion chatting, while I ate ramen noodles and mixing-bowl-sized servings of Cap'n Crunch cereal. With each new person, I made up a different age, name, and location. I could be anyone. Typically, I called myself Keisha, Latonya, or Toya; something like my real name, in case we happened to meet in person. Each new notification from someone looking to chat cut through the silence of my empty apartment. I lived and breathed for the AOL message notification. The chatroom replaced my relationships with friends, peers, and church members. I had an excess of time, wild and frenzied curiosity, and zero accountability.

I thought of Darryl, Maurice, Anthony, and Kelvin. They had all failed me in one way or another. I felt if I had met one man, I'd met them all. After Kelvin, I couldn't bear the thought of being involved sexually with another man. I recoiled at the thought of one touching me. Still desiring affection, I joined chatrooms for women who were lesbian, bi-curious, or interested in platonic friendships. I wrote introductions like "AA female, bi-curious, looking for friends." Other times I wrote, "AA curvy female looking for discreet, no-strings-attached fun." But what I meant was, "AA female seeking friendship, relationships, or family—but will have sex or enter into a relationship if you want." I wanted the people I met online to somehow help me feel wanted and more human.

I was eager to find out if being with a woman would help me feel again. I lost time imagining what it would feel like to walk hand-in-hand at the mall, sit across the table from someone at a restaurant, and have someone to join me in the middle of the dance floor laughing as we drunkenly gyrated to '90s R&B. I dreamed of being in love with my best friend, a feminine woman like myself. In her presence, insecurity about my body would dissipate. We could share everything with each other.

One Sunday at a time, I isolated myself from my friends Stephanie and Harold and others in my church community. When invites came to visit her and her family, I declined. My church attendance, which had been weekly, became once or twice a month at best. I feared they would see the change in me. When my friends and fellow church members said anything negative about gays and lesbians, I took offense and further distanced myself—without explanation. Most church members and heterosexual military members dismissed and ignorantly labeled my lifestyle as a *sickness*—something to be cured, cleansed, suppressed. Every church I attended from childhood through adulthood, whether Missionary Baptist, Pentecostal, Free Will Baptist, or Nondenominational, preached sermons against homosexuality. In my experience as a member of these congregations, homosexuality and abortion were the biggest sins.

"God made Adam and Eve, *not* Adam and Steve!" the pastor yelled. "The Bible says we are all born into sin, but we DON'T have to stay that way. Will the church say 'amen'?" He banged his hand against his Bible. "The sanctity of marriage is under attack and people are engaging in unnatural relationships. It's all over the TV. God said man shall find a wife, *not* another man!"

As he spoke, I felt the sting of condemnation in the pit of my stomach. I rolled my eyes and scrolled past the members of the congregation, all nodding and throwing their hands in the air. "Amen, pastor! Preach!"

God, please change me. I prayed day and night, fearing my lifestyle would send me to Hell. If I exposed my true self, my church friends would lose respect for me. Too many times, I'd heard them debate about how they would feel if they had a gay son or daughter—whether they could still love their child, whether they could still accept their child into their home, whether they could have a friend who identified as gay.

"I don't care, as long as they don't come on to me."

"I can't have a lesbian being friends with my wife. That's like inviting the devil into our home."

"I don't know what I would do if one of my kids ended up gay. I would be devastated. I would still love them, but I don't know if we could have a relationship."

"Being gay is a serious sin because it's an outward sin—everyone knows about it. And you can't get rid of it like other sins. You have to suppress your urges, live a life of celibacy if you want to be accepted by God."

Their comments, all said in earnest, told me I wouldn't be accepted if I identified as a lesbian. I said nothing during these conversations, which didn't feel right. Hearing their various comments gave me the impression that if they knew of my same-sex attractions, they would abandon me like everyone else in my life had. I didn't want to be alienated from the only people who accepted the part of me they knew.

Within weeks of ending the marriage with Kelvin, I drove an hour from Mountain Home Air Force Base to Boise, so I could spend time with LGBTQIA friends and partners. While I was in public at the mall, restaurants, or clubs, I scanned the crowd, making sure I wouldn't be seen by anyone I knew. Identifying as a gay or lesbian military member in the early 2000s came with shame and forced outing by chains of command. The "Don't Ask, Don't Tell" policy worked to effectively discharge any person who did not identify as heterosexual. By acting on my attraction, I risked being targeted and kicked out of the military. After the Monday morning roll call, where we stood at parade rest to have our uniforms inspected and listen to our squadron commander make morning announcements, small talk ensued and everyone shared highlights from the weekend. I felt isolated and ashamed of my secrets as everyone else openly discussed their weekends. One person had driven home to see their parents, another had attended a BBQ with a group of friends. When coworkers looked at me to participate, I made up stories about how I'd spent the weekend clean-ing. I couldn't say, "I went to see a drag show and went on a date with my girlfriend." I couldn't be myself—at the time, I didn't even know myself.

For about two years, I had a series of one-night stands and short-term relationships. The first relationship stemmed from early chats via AOL. We discussed sex first, and the conversations then moved to private messaging for several days. Once we were comfortable with each other, we agreed to meet at Target. Emily arrived in the shoe department at our agreed-upon time. She was a curvaceous woman in her thirties with waist-length brown hair and outgrown blonde highlights. She looked just like her picture. She described herself as biracial, being part Shoshone tribe and part Scottish. Emily wore a long-sleeved maxi dress, brown clogs, and amethyst jewelry. When she smiled, her dimples almost covered her entire cheek. She first introduced me to sushi, Mad Dog 20/20, and a woman who ate her own placenta shortly after giving birth to her son, River.

For one of our dates, we went on a picnic in the park—my first picnic. She told me about her years of being a band groupie, getting high on heroin, and spending months in rehab. She had other stories about the times she met James Brown and Michael Jackson. She told her friends about me, calling me *beautiful* and *sexy*. She introduced me to Kama Sutra. She also allowed me to fumble my way around her body, an experience I never quite conquered. Still, she stayed with me and cried when I refused to commit. She spoke often about us building our lives together, whether I decided to stay in the military or not. She cooked for me, called multiple times a day, and introduced me to her family. On more than one occasion, I ghosted her, refused to accept her calls, and stopped talking to her altogether. She emailed me love letters, surprised me at home, and begged me to come back. I hated how much she loved me. How dare she love a woman who didn't know how to love herself *or* love her in return. I felt underserving of her affection.

There were also shorter encounters, none lasting as long as my relationship with Emily. None of my relationships worked because I grew sick of hiding, lying, and of being an imposter. I ghosted a lot of people, and they didn't know why. I hurt a lot of people—good friends and partners who deserved to be loved. But I didn't know how to be emotionally available. The relationships failed because of my own fear, shame, and immaturity. A lot of women cared about me, and some fell in love. They spoke of plans to one day live together, be married, raise children.

Years later, I delved deeper into the root of my attraction to women. Wholeness comes with first understanding *why*. My attraction began at an early age from the one-time experience with Danielle. I also thought my relationships with women would fill my need for affection, safety, and belonging. At the time, I believed no man could fulfill my emotional needs— I did not feel safe with men. I wanted someone to hold me, wipe my tears, acknowledge and celebrate my success, and spend time with me. Each relationship, each sexual partner, was an illegitimate cure for legitimate injuries.

I longed for each new partner the way I had longed for a mommy and daddy. Although I grew up knowing and living with my mother, we didn't have a bonded relationship, so I felt like a motherless child. Although I grew up with knowledge of a man's name inked on my birth certificate and carried his last name, I felt like a fatherless child. Each sexual partner represented the number of times my brother had touched me and my mother had hit me, the number of times I had longed for my father to hold me.

I used sex to receive affection—it's the only way I knew. My body could do things my emotions couldn't. But because sex was the main topic in church, I downplayed my desire for representation, connection, affection, validation, and security. The message I received at church was you're *in* God's will, or you're *out* of God's will. You're either *in* with your church family, or you're an outsider, rebel, sinner. I would later grow to understand the errors of this black and white thinking. You're straight, or you're headed to hell. Either you're one of us, or you're a worldly sinner. Your choice ..., *choice* being the key word.

CHAPTER 38

Likable or No?

"We are afraid to care too much, for fear that the other person does not care at all."

~ELEANOR ROOSEVELT

Everyone I met scared me. Still, I hungered for nothing more than authentic, close-knit friendships. But could a wounded girl like me have a real relationship? I fully believed each person would hurt me when I least suspected it. I was always convinced something was wrong with the other person. As the self-fulfilling prophecy goes, I proved myself correct. I convinced myself that my relationships with potential friends and romantic partners were *not* real, and they would abandon me at some point;

often, they did. I feared allowing anyone to know the real me. I thought, *What if I tell them I'm alienated from my family? Will they blame me for not trying hard enough? What if I tell them about my sexual improprieties? Will they look at me differently, the way that people who disagree with gay relationships look disapprovingly, disgustingly at gay people? And if I tell them about how I tried to kill myself on more than one occasion, will they call me crazy and distance themselves?*

I tried to remind myself about the dangers of fear, and how it can suck the life out of us if we let it. And how fear can keep us from living the life we are destined to live. I tried to remind myself not to fear authentic relationships and vulnerability, but I'd been hurt too much.

I didn't have examples of strong female relationships during my childhood. I did not have many friends, did not belong to clubs or cliques. Growing up, I had more conversations inside my head than with other people. This set the stage for difficulty as an adult. As an adult, having a connection with other women meant being accepted. It meant I mattered—finally. Someone once told me that friendship is love with skin on it. Friendship is love. My favorite movies, such as *Fried Green Tomatoes* and *Waiting to Exhale*, were examples of love. Both movies depict friendship as having close emotional bonds, with physical closeness, listening, talking, crying together, laughing together, celebrating together, fighting for one another, and supporting each other. The women in both movies journey through life's ups and downs—together. The friendships were unbreakable. I knew these relationships existed because I'd been in close proximity to women who had found their person or their tribe, yet I hadn't found my own.

I fed the insecurity by thinking of myself as too awkward, too damaged, and having nothing to offer. The events of my childhood told me love wasn't meant for me. I distanced myself from Momma for years because I believed she no longer loved me. I convinced myself that my aunts, who supported and mentored me when I was a child, did not truly care for me. I believed having the love of family and friends was meant for others. The walls I built to keep from being rejected also prevented me from having genuine connections.

Each woman I met represented my mother; I saw all of them as people who would eventually leave or abuse me. After I survived the suicide attempt, I changed my number as a way of saying goodbye to everyone in Idaho, including Stephanie. Although she'd been there to help me select a wedding ring and had also been there on both my wedding day, and the day I shot myself, I convinced myself she would turn her back on me. I fully believed she would get too busy with her life to be there for me. I stopped all communication prior to relocating to North Carolina. She didn't change—I did. We reconnected years later, but too much time had passed for us to regain the friendship we'd once had. She'd been a friend and spiritual mentor, and I let her slip away.

Years later, I would meet Heather and Mark. Heather was a sharp-tongued Louisiana native who wore her husband's oversized work shirts, hated dogs, and loved home improvement projects. Mark was a passive, quiet guy from Honduras. He was also an Air Force veteran and an electrician who liked Ford Mustangs. We drank, cooked, and held game nights in our homes. One night, I sat in Heather's office creating a résumé for Mark. As she vented about her relationship with Mark and previous, abusive marriage, I felt compelled to share about my own relationships including the history of one-night stands and same-sex relationships. When I told Heather, she looked shocked. She didn't say anything except, "Wow." After a week of not speaking, she told me Mark didn't want her to be friends with me anymore. Prior to that conversation, we had not argued, broken each other's trust, or done anything to hurt or disrespect each other. I couldn't help but wonder if my revelation had changed the way she felt. Ending our friendship hurt even more because we had spoken to one another almost daily. I had been there when she had her first child, and I had planned her baby shower. She had helped me celebrate my birthday and had comforted me many times when I needed a shoulder to cry on.

I made another friend, Bianca, while I was on active duty and stationed at Pope Air Force Base. I'd pass her office, which was near Logistics, and heard her laughing with her coworkers. One day I decided to stop in and introduce myself. Daily visits became routine and, like I had with Heather and Mark, I bonded with Bianca almost immediately. We discussed past intimate relationships, work, faith in God, and family upbringing. Bianca was the kind of woman whose strong voice didn't match her five-foot height. She was married to Damon, an active duty member who was a foot taller than her. Together they parented three kids. Bianca had experienced great loss after several miscarriages and stillbirths. During that time, she confided in me, as she grieved each loss.

Like me, she also weathered a difficult marriage due to infidelity. During this challenging time, we remained close—I thought. But as Bianca's relationship with her husband began to heal, our communication lessened. After the devastating loss of one of her infant children, she refrained from inviting me to the funeral. Soon after, Bianca and her husband relocated out of state, and she did not so much as send a text message to say goodbye. Years later, after we found one another on Facebook, she sent me a private message: "I'm sorry for isolating myself after Zachary's passing. We were tight."

But certainly, there had to have been a reason she said *goodbye* in such a pointed way. She'd kept in contact with other coworkers, and they would pass on updates. Even after the apology, I couldn't help but blame myself. I'd shared so much with Bianca. Did I open up to her too much? Did I offend or hurt her in some way? I'd hoped she would be honest with me and tell me if she felt that I'd been a terrible friend, but the explanation for her ghosting never came. After so many failed relationships, I'm sure I played a part. I only wished I knew how so I could take responsibility, apologize, and make it right.

The end of one relationship always made it that much harder to welcome another. I often wondered if I'd mistaken work friends for *real* friends. Staring at my reflection, I imagined words written on my forehead with a thick black sharpie: "CAUTION—DAMAGED GOODS. NEEDY. DO NOT BEFRIEND." Lonely people always wait to be recognized. I waited for women, who I thought were friends, to invite me to lunch, house-warming parties, birthday celebrations, girls' trips, and nights out. I lost trust in my ability to maintain long-term relationships. Each time a relationship ended, it felt like a bloody wound that would never heal. Each time, it hurt a hundred times more than the pain I'd experienced as a child because these new losses were women I'd chosen to have in my life, and I assumed they'd also chosen me— but they all scattered like leaves on a windy day.

Whenever I found someone to call my *friend*, I'd lose myself by going over and above what's required for a normal friendship. I have a history of acting as the savior in my relationships. All my friendships revolved around family crises, domestic violence, relationship stress, or life-altering events. Because I was too familiar with abandonment, I forced relationships with people who I viewed as being able to relate to my history. I will admit to being needy in the way I visited, texted, and called daily. I will admit that I used friendships to replace lost family connections. My lack of boundaries and balance created resentment. My perception of the hard work I put into each relationship caused me to feel taken for granted.

I didn't give a single person time to earn the right to be called a *friend*—each one received the title like an honorary degree. For years, I was confused about the meaning of *friend*, both what it meant to have and to be one.

I believed that in order to have a friend, I needed to be the person I've always wanted in my life. I tried to make myself into the mother, sister, aunt, and neighbor I once needed. At the time, I couldn't see the future. But I would become the mother, sister, and woman I longed to have in my own life. I focused my energy solely on what I needed, instead of what my friend needed. If I sat with her heartbreak, I thought she might sit with mine. My failed relationships all fell into the same six stages.

Stage One: Wonder. I was giddy with excitement about embarking on a new relationship. We'd laugh, converse about shared interests, and text or talk regularly. There wasn't a day that would go by when my friend didn't cross my mind. We'd talk, text, or see each other daily. I'd say to myself, "Finally."

Stage Two: Work. I'd make myself available for everything. I'd answer calls and texts immediately. I'd do favors, even when I didn't want to. When she was in crisis, I was there to respond. I wanted to fix the problem instead of just listening. I'd lend money, babysit her children, move furniture, make her soup when she was sick, and prepare a medicine goodie bag. Within a few weeks or months of getting to know her, I'd invite her to my home, and we would celebrate birthdays and holidays together.

I'd overshare about my life. I'd ignore the voice telling me to be cautious.

Stage Three: Intuition. This stage occurred within the first six to twelve months. I'd take notice of all the ways I was trying too hard. I'd be the therapist, cook, babysitter, and overall problem-solver. I'd ask myself, "Where is she when I need a hand?"

Stage Four: Fight. By this stage, I'd grow tired, resentful, and angry. The relationship would be on its last leg, but I'd do anything within my power to prevent the end. The distance between us would grow deeper with each passing week. I'd strategize ways to salvage the break by texting, visiting, and sending invites for dinner. I'd ask her often, "Where have you been? Why haven't we talked?" I'd beg for answers.

Stage Five: Victimization. I'd be in denial about my role in the break. I'd beg God for answers. I'd also cry, sulk, and withdraw from the online and physical worlds.

Stage Six: Acceptance. I'd get on with the business of living. I'd review the relationship's timeline. Friendships fuel me, even though I didn't know how women maintained long lasting relationships. Once I evaluated my short-comings, I opened up to others and started the process again.

* * *

During years of therapy, my therapist forced me to acknowledge my history of toxic relationship habits.

Therapy helped me realize other people are *not* the source of my issues; I'm the reason my relationships don't last. I didn't use any stages of the relationship to get to know the other person. I rushed to build my friendships without knowing if we were a good fit. But because of therapy, I learned it is not my job to control, fix, or save people. I learned to question my motives and intentions. Almost all of my relationships began after I heard my friend had experienced misfortune. In my counterproductive attempts to ingratiate myself to a new friendship to a degree that was often interpreted as *overeager*, I often said, "yes" out of fear that if I didn't, my friends wouldn't love me. I feared they would abandon the relationships. While I took responsibility for my part in relationships ending, I also realized it was my habit to attract female friends who liked my advice, sense of humor, home, food, and time—but didn't like nor want *all* of me.

CHAPTER 39

All of Me

"It takes courage to grow up and turn out to be who you really are."

~E.E. CUMMINGS

There are three distinct parts of me. Maybe it's better to say, there are three of ME. The *first* me, the one who existed before I was sexually assaulted, hadn't heard the word "sex" or the correct anatomical names for her body parts. She didn't know what she didn't know. She wore rompers, pigtails, and Velcro-fastened sneakers. She sang, as she counted her ten fingers and ten toes, and she loved *Rapunzel* and *The Three Little Pigs*. She loved playtime, bath time, and laughter. Most photos reveal her brandishing big brown eyes and a mischievous smile. She loved to be tickled and gave hugs as big as her arms would stretch. She loved her family. She is the best version of me.

After being sexually assaulted, the *second* me couldn't find anywhere to hide or anyone to trust. She existed but didn't know how to live. From ages eight to seventeen, she tried her best to stay hidden. She questioned whether every adult was either an abuser or a victim and didn't believe there was any place in between. She wanted affection but feared physical and emotional closeness. She struggled to recognize good people or good times; they were few and far between. She was aware that nothing in this world belonged to her, most of all, her body. She looked clean and well-nurtured—but she wore abandonment like skin. She was an alien with no language to describe what had transpired. How could she tell people she was dying, when no one had stopped to notice the signs? She wanted to love and be loved, but she was certain love was not meant for her. She believed she was too damaged to be of any good, like trash unloaded at the landfill. She prayed for death to come—a gift for surviving the pain. She carried this prayer, this anger, this loneliness daily. Each day, and its happenings were a blur. There was little to nothing that was sacred. That girl was sure she'd die before her nineteenth birthday.

The *third* me is a fully-grown woman who looks back at the other two as a testament to who I was then, always reminding myself of the distance I've traveled since. Though I am always and forever grateful for the life I now possess, I sometimes want to be that first incarnation of me again—the one with the care-free laughter and freedom. I long for this *first* me to infuse every aspect of my current day-to-day adult life. Sometimes I long for her unadulterated, clean mind and her pure naïveté. I want to protect and hold the *second* me with all the knowledge and experience that I've acquired since. I long to give her all the love that she so longed for but was deprived of. I want to assure her life will and does get better. I want to love her and keep her on a path to wellness, instead of exposing her to the hardship that almost annihilated her. Today, all parts of who I am are accepted and loved. I am profoundly grateful to be a living testimony of service to the world today.

CHAPTER 40

Aha Moment

"For I know the plans I have for you," declares the LORD,
"plans to prosper you and not to harm you, plans to give you
hope and a future."

~JEREMIAH 29:11 (NIV)

I still remember the particular Sunday when, at the age of twelve, I gave my life to Christ and professed my need for a higher power. I knew even then that this Sunday would be immeasurably different. I would be saved. Wearing my favorite black-and-pink paisley dress and matching hot-pink Mary Jane flats, I stood before my mother early this Sunday morning, awaiting her inspection before church. "Why do you always wear that damn dress?"

It was a question I hadn't expected her to ask. I thought I looked pretty, and I felt even better. The dress and matching shoes were one of the few things I owned that aligned with my personal style. When Katrina turned to walk away, I returned to my closet to look at my options and debated changing. I didn't want Katrina to berate me again on the same day.

I'd spent the past week praying and reading the Bible, trying to understand the Book of Revelations. I questioned eternity, and where I might spend it when I die. After arriving to church, I walked into the sanctuary and paid attention to the wall plaques that listed church attendance, new members, and the number of people who had been saved the previous Sunday. My friends and I took our places along an oak veneer pew. My hands shook, as I thought about walking in front of the congregation to state my desire to be baptized. The pastor's fiery sermon presented us with the option to change our lives or leave service as sinners headed to hell.

Worrying I would be late and wouldn't have the chance to declare my faith again, I began my walk to the front of the church. Everything felt like it was happening in slow motion, as I waited for my turn to speak. Present that day were faithful churchgoers I recognized from week to week as well as some backsliders. Standing in front of others and making a declaration of my faith felt awkward and unreasonable—but it's what the church required. We all took our turns stating our intentions to get baptized, repent our sins, or join the church. When the pastor held the mic in front of me, I said, "I want to be baptized."

The previous week, about ten of my church friends had done the same and gotten baptized that day. Not wanting to submit to peer pressure, I decided to wait a week. This early choice became the catalyst for my thoughts about religion. I longed to be a part of a spiritual body where I would be accepted for who I was. I also wanted the freedom to find and to speak my truth. But how could the most difficult, embarrassing parts of my story be shared with those who shared my faith? Though I regularly attended church while living with Katrina, I didn't yet understand my life as its own beautiful testimony. I was too busy trying to survive.

As an adult, when I reflect on the different congregations I've been a part of throughout my walk with God, many churches fell short of my needs and expectations. In my dreams, I often get a glimpse of the church I would one day like to attend: a truly nonjudgmental grace-filled church. It is an intimate setting with a culturally and racially diverse congregation, with leadership that mirrors its diversity. We would all be set free by our ability to be openly frank and honest. We'd support social justice, advocacy, and open our doors to strangers.

If I were to be baptized again today, I would envision myself standing at a candlelit pulpit dressed casually in a white tee, a sheer black kimono, ripped jeans, and sandals. I would be before the congregation about to share my testimony, nervous but filled to the brim, full with love and positive energy. The congregation would be sitting in silence, praying for me, before I even uttered one word. As congregants, we are all bonded by the belief that we are all God's people, equally accepted regardless of our past and present circumstances. I see myself sharing truths about my past, including my attempted suicide and my struggles with understanding my sexuality. In my dreams, people get it. They get me and accept me. Our bonds grow stronger, and others follow suit to share their own redemption story.

I've belonged to churches that followed a script I didn't have within my reach and could not abide to. I vividly recall standing among my peers during praise and worship, praying for God to touch me with the gift of speaking in tongues. I tried it on my own, hoping God would bless my mumbling, tongue-tied speech, asking, *Is this it, God?* If God granted me the holy language, then and only then would I consider myself a real Christian.

I lost myself trying to emulate a standard upheld by others. Church cliques and school cliques seemed identical. Both taught me to hide the truth about myself. I listened to the way church members discussed anyone classified as *other* when they said things like, "Girl, did you see that dress Misty wore? Could it have been any tighter?" And during the sermons, the pastor chastised young men with feminine characteristics by saying, "God can heal anything, including homosexuality."

What I observed in church didn't mirror what I'd read about Jesus. He welcomed, encouraged, led, prayed, healed, and fed people. Reading my Bible gave me clarity about my role as a Christian. I realized I am called to be like Jesus.

I'm endowed with the power to use the gifts, talents, and resources God provides, and it's my hope that each of us would arrive at this *aha* moment. We are the answers to the world's problems. We are the healers, deliverers, and miracle workers we've been waiting for. We are the answers to the world's questions and to every dilemma known to man. We can embody the good news and minister to others, just as Jesus did for all of us. We can even stop the cycle of abuse in our families and communities.

When healing is our priority, we can get honest about our truth. My truth is that I was born to a mother who is incapable of loving me. I grew up as a daddy-less daughter. My own brother, who should have protected me and been an ally to me, sexually abused me. I grew into adulthood feeling alone, ugly, worthless, pitiful, and out of place in the world. My truth is that my family did not love me in the way I needed to be loved. Because of this, I over-shopped, over-sexed, over-drank, over-ate, and over-medicated to compensate for every painful memory and insecurity. I allowed fear to control my life. This led to difficulties in maintaining healthy relationships.

But here's the other truth: I should not be alive after shooting myself. Being real is more important than appearing strong. Today I'm a wife, mother, veteran, college graduate, writer, mental health advocate, speaker, and friend. I am so abundantly glad to be alive today. I've asked God to let my legacy live on and reverberate in each and every life I'm blessed enough to touch now and long after I'm gone.

I still battle with insecurities and often still contend with old ways of thinking. *No one loves you. You're worthless.* When these thoughts surface, I'm able to let them pass. I'm able to recognize them as an old script that has never served me well. The thoughts come when I'm alone or experiencing the end of a friendship. Loneliness is an old companion and an emotion I've felt more often than joy, love, peace, or happiness. But that's changing now.

After spending a lifetime praying, I needed someone to be an answer to my prayer. I needed love. I needed people who would stand by my side as witnesses to both my painful and joyful experiences. The cure to loneliness is for all of us to use our gifts, skills, and abilities to become role models, friends, mentors, and helpers to each other. Using our God-given personalities, talents, and resources, we can do a small part in stopping the cycle of abuse from tormenting those we know and love. I don't want to ever be complicit (directly or indirectly) in the suffering of others. Many of us are suffering in silence, waiting for someone to give a damn. We are hoping that someone will come along and call, text, or reach out to us. Just like Momma picked me up when Katrina left me on the porch, we all need to be picked up and nourished emotionally, physically, and spiritually. Each of our lives is finite; we only have a short time to make an impact, but the opportunities to make a difference in our families and our communities is boundless.

CHAPTER 41

Hope

"When I think about the people I admire most, with histories of overcoming difficult childhoods, they are proof that if God can do that for them, He can certainly do the same for me."

~ME

When I was six years old, Momma told me God was going to use me. Her words were so necessary, so timely— she said this right before jarring and devastating changes. At eight, my brother molested me, and my mother began beating me. By then, I prayed daily for God to take my life. By twenty-one, I attempted to take my own life. Almost twenty years have passed since that time. Nothing about my life has been easy. Healing takes a lifetime, and perhaps it's meant to be that way.

Loneliness is an automatic trigger for old thinking patterns in which I believe that my life is of little importance to others. But when those moments come now, I don't automatically think of killing myself the way I used to. I mentally list the people who love me unconditionally, the people who would miss me if I were gone, and the people who have demonstrated to me they care for me deeply. I remember the good as much as I can and remind myself every day that I live a life that is more peaceful and blessed than I could have ever imagined possible.

I didn't get everything that I've always wanted. I've been angry with God in each season of my life because I didn't receive the family or the sense of belonging I prayed for and thought I needed. Instead, God helped me to redefine who and what I need. God gave me the family that brought me to this book *and* to you—to other people who understand what it feels like to be left out. This book was created for you.

You may wonder how I got from there to here. The answers are complicated. Therapy helped. I decided to pursue it after I separated from the Air Force. I found a therapist with whom I felt comfortable sharing the secrets I'd held my whole life. She gave me straightforward, no-nonsense feedback. The first two years of therapy helped me to process all the thoughts and feelings I hadn't been able to share with anyone. During my sessions, the therapist said, "You're not crazy, you're traumatized."

She led me to clearly see the link between my history of trauma and my persistent symptoms of post-traumatic stress disorder. She allowed me to breathe air into the parts of my soul that I had abandoned—no, forgotten. I'd forgotten to give myself grace for the mistakes and bad decisions I'd made, but therapy helped me learn to accept both the good and the not-so-good parts of myself. I learned to see myself through the eyes of others and respond to compliments. Instead of turning away or ignoring kind gestures, I learned to say, "thank you." The therapist helped me learn how to say "no" and slowly decrease my people-pleasing habits. In truth, I'm still learning the power of a simple "no." Therapy taught me about PTSD and how it relates to my decision making, poor relationship history, and fight-or-flight responses. Therapy taught me how to be emotionally, physically, and spiritually kind and gentle to myself. I learned to understand my chest pains, panicked feelings, and racing heart palpitations—all of which have been present since childhood—as symptoms of panic attacks resulting from trauma. I feel better having a name and a reason for my experiences.

Faith and hope have helped. I wouldn't have gotten to this place of acceptance without years of disciplined, internal work. Over time, I moved away from rehashing every horrible, demeaning event and started keeping the good in mind. Several years ago, I began a daily routine of watching pastor Joel Osteen and retraining my depressing thoughts. Each night, before bed, I grab my journal and list at least ten things that I feel are blessings. Most days, I write the same entries over and over. On August 26, 2007, I wrote my first entry in the journal my husband purchased for me:

Ten Things to Be Thankful For:

1.   *My house—it's my first home.*

2.   *My health.*

3.   *Good neighbors—no violence, a good place to raise a family.*

4.   *A great husband and daughter—he is amazing, and she loves me.*

5.   *Transportation.*

6.   *Money.*

7.   *Education—I got further than I ever thought I would.*

8.   *My in-laws.*

9.   *This morning, I had anxiety—before long, I felt better.*

10. *Music*

Each year that passes is another year I celebrate being farther removed from my painful childhood. I've overcome several challenges that accompany growing up without parental and family support. The scars from the self-inflicted gunshot wound remain. It's a reminder of events I wish I could forget. It's also a reminder of how desperately I want to live.

* * *

My mental and professional journeys merged when I went from attempting to take my life to having a job as the Patient Safety Program Manager at Seymour Johnson Air Force Base. From 2010 through 2017, I have investigated how and why active duty members commit suicide.

At each stage, and with each marker of success, I questioned whether I deserved the achievement. Today I hold five college degrees. This comes after being a failing student in high school. Academic achievement meant proving to myself that I have the mental and intellectual capacity to learn and to retain knowledge. I'm proud of who I've become in this capacity, and my degrees have served me professionally and personally in ways I'd never imagined. My own pain from childhood trauma led me into the mental health field, where I am now a mental health therapist. I am not embarrassed to say I see my own pain in the lives of my clients. They are a reminder of what I survived. They help me to remember the things that children never forget. I advocate for my clients who are victims of abuse and neglect. Had I successfully ended my life, I wouldn't be able to teach others how to save themselves, how to parent themselves, how to accept themselves, and how to love themselves, unapologetically.

If I had killed myself, I wouldn't have been able to teach others how to find their voice, communicate their needs, or go after their goals.

I found a way to channel my disappointment through my work—each session, each child, one life at a time. That's the purpose my grandmother told me about. That's what she meant when she said, "God is going to use you." As a mental health professional, I find myself offering hope to my clients in much of the same way. My hope is that anyone who struggles with the effects of trauma will find the strength to keep living. Pain can be used for a greater purpose. Life gets better when *we* get better.

Remembering that Katrina is human has helped. I used to see her as a demon, a psychotic freak, and a terrorist. I am still working to see her differently—as deeply flawed, deeply traumatized, and not up to the task of changing or ending her own pain to prevent debilitating others. I grieve only for the things I never had with her, like a mother-daughter relationship. I have no desire to have her in my life today. Being unloved by so many has taught me to love hard and fearlessly.

CHAPTER 42

The One

I moved from believing no one would love me prior to my first marriage to falling deeply in love just a few years after I almost ended my life. Today, my husband has known me longer than my family did. While we were getting to know each other, before we decided to cement our relationship, I shared with him my history of child abuse. He held in his hands the letters Katrina wrote to the Air Force and read them all. I replayed the voicemail she left, taunting me by saying, "You black bitch, you can't get away from me. If I ever see you again, I will kill you." Saddened, he looked up at me and said, "What mother would do this?"

Our courtship lasted three years, and one of the most memorable birthdays I've ever had was one Chris and I celebrated together on August 13th, 2004. By this point in our courtship, Chris had proved himself to be trustworthy of my affection and adoration. We were in love.

At the time, he lived an hour away, and we alternated weekend visits with one another. Waiting for his arrival, butterflies danced in my stomach. He arrived in his F150 truck, and I ran outside when I heard the sound of his truck's engine. Seeing him and laughing with him was my favorite time after a long, exhausting week. Upon seeing me, he smiled his gorgeous smile and exclaimed, "Look what I got for you."

In the front seat were one, two, no *three* boxes wrapped with curled, red ribbon and handwritten messages on white and blue wrapping paper, which I've still saved to this day. Sixteen years into our marriage, I still read these love notes with pride, gratitude, and joy. The messages read, "You're beautiful, and the smartest woman I know. I love your eyes. You make me so happy." Still, others boldly stated, "I want to spend the rest of my life with you. Our love for each other is a beautiful thing." The message that moved me most read, "Everything I do, everything I am, and everything good in my life is that much sweeter with you in my life. You are my best friend and my everything. Seeing that beautiful smile on your face is all I need. You're going to be my wife one day."

Each carefully wrapped box contained a unique pair of Chuck Taylor tennis shoes—each a different design and color. One pair was the classic black and white, another was denim with a maroon and cream vintage design, and the third pair was pink! I marvel at how he understood my personal taste so well. He also gifted me with the softest teddy bear I'd ever held, and while he was deployed I held the bear in remembrance of his embrace.

Along with the shoes and cuddly teddy bear, he gave me a beautiful bouquet of white and yellow roses and a chocolate cake—chocolate was my absolute favorite. We spent the rest of the evening at home, and I wept tears of joy. I cried—A LOT. I couldn't believe someone had made such a big deal out of my born day. I couldn't fathom the thought, planning, and the money he'd spent on ME. I couldn't believe he drove an hour after work to celebrate the day to then spend the weekend with me. In this tenderest of moments, the previous birthdays which didn't get celebrated didn't matter much. Plus, I finally reveled in receiving the handwritten notes and birthday cake I'd always wanted. His love healed me.

* * *

I recall vividly the moment I knew I wanted to spend the rest of my life with him. Driving my car towards the front gate of the base, I thought about the day I had told him everything—my entire past—and he said, "I still want you." He wanted me with all my baggage. He wanted *me*. I knew from that point on that he was my *Mr. Right*; he was *The One*. "I don't want anyone else," I said aloud with God as my witness. Having him by my side these past seventeen years has been the greatest blessing of my life, and I couldn't imagine anyone else by my side on this life-long journey.

I could never have predicted I would fall in love so deeply and so completely, and be able to experience the joys of having that love requited with the man who would become my indispensable spouse. Loving him has also meant knowing the joy of being a mother to his daughter—no, *our* daughter, Kya. I was blessed to be there for her on her first day of Kindergarten, the day she started her menstrual cycle, the day she moved into her college dorm—and other important milestones like learning to drive. Thanks to her, I love Disney movies, *Sponge Bob*, and *The Backyardigans*. She is smarter than both of us and is often outspoken, quick-witted, thoughtful, and empathetic. Our home is the hang-out spot for her group of friends. Our home has hosted countless sleepovers and bonfires. One of the most special times that we share is when we are in the kitchen cooking dinner and baking cakes. She is already a better baker than I in some capacities. She is a patient cook, whereas I want to speed up the process, hurry, and get it done.

She is blessed with many talents. She gave me the opportunity to be *piano lesson mom, soccer mom, basketball mom, theater mom, gymnastics mom, Booster Club mom,* and *volleyball* —*MOM*. She knows my history and shares in the retelling of my story, without falling victim to its sorrow. She knows about my struggle, but because she knows she's fully protected and loved, it's possible for her to act as both a witness *and* a bedrock to me. When she hugs

me, calls me, tells me she loves me—like her father, she
is healing me *still*. We have deep conversations, and my
heart is filled to the brim when she shares the details of
her day. In our living room sits a plaque I received from
her for Christmas that reads *Best Mom Ever.* I am a wife,
mom, and friend. I am chosen and loved. I am forever a
part of her growth and her future, as she is forever a part
of my health and my recovery.

CHAPTER 43

You Matter

"You have a voice. You have a choice. You Matter!"

~ME

A lot of us have grown up in families where we were raised by grandmas, aunties, and other people—maybe we were abandoned by our immediate family or estranged from them. Maybe we grew up surrounded by people who didn't know how to love us correctly or didn't live up to our expectations of what love should be. Maybe they weren't loved well either and neglected by those who were central to their own lives. Maybe there was the shame of sexual, physical, or emotional abuse which handicapped their ability to receive love and give love in return.

Know implicitly and deep down in the core of your own personal truth, that the acts committed against us do not define who we are, or who we can become. The people who abused us do not get the last word on our personal happiness or the quality of life we deserve for ourselves. The people who are absent, silent, dismissive, and complicit in our oppression —they don't define who we are. The friends who do not stick around don't define us, either. Our lives are not dependent on people who aren't there. Our past does not dictate our belonging in the universe. You deserve to be here. You deserve to be loved well. You matter.

Most of us have heard the saying "time heals." We hear it most often when we're grieving; people try to comfort us by telling us that one day things won't hurt as much. People said it to me, but it was a lie. It hurt twenty, thirty years ago—and it hurts today. Maybe I would have healed if the people who hurt me had acknowledged their part in my suffering. But that wasn't my experience. Time gave me a chance to find new meaning in the events that transpired. It allowed me to see the people in my life differently, and within a new context of being able to reflect thoughtfully on past events with an insight I didn't have at the time I was first experiencing them. It allowed me to separate myself from the events that hurt me and see myself as more than the *abused*. Those things happened to me, but they're *not* who I am.

The abuse does not define me; my ability to define myself in light of my abuse put me back in the driver's seat and proved to me, once and for all, how resourceful I am. In time, I have become my own best advocate. With the fruition of time, I now live the life I've always wanted. I've sought out the experiences that I needed which were essential to my recovery. In the twenty or so years since I left Arkansas and Colorado, I've learned to celebrate myself, forgive myself, and accept myself.

We are born with what I like to refer to as a *life script*. We are told who we should be, and what we should believe—and often, how we should feel. Here's what I need you to understand. If you have hope, you can overcome unimaginable, seemingly insurmountable circumstances. With hope, you can create your own script and decide what you want to do with your life. Just because your life starts one way, that doesn't mean it has to end the same way. Stay hopeful and authentic about how you feel, and what you've been through.

Eventually, all of us must confront the pain which limits us—and we do this by first acknowledging its detrimental presence in our lives. We chip away at it by sharing our pain with people who have proven to be safe guardians worthy of hearing our stories. We face our pain by sharing our testimony of overcoming our lifelong struggles in schools, churches, conferences, and—when appropriate—on social media. When we share our pain, we help to erase the shame and the stigma attached to mental illness and trauma-related experiences. From there, we can move forward and get on with the business of living, growing, and most importantly, loving.

As I sit in my recliner, I'm preparing for work tomorrow by thinking of the needs of my clients. The families I work with each have distinct needs. Some need food, others a new home after surviving a fire, and still others need medical attention. It's my job to connect them to what they need while also offering a safe place for them to talk about their life experiences which most often have been impacted by trauma. In this way, I can say that I'm being used to positively impact adults, children, and families. I'm living proof that insurmountable circumstances can be overcome with hope, inspiration, and the refusal to give up.

* * *

Momma, who passed away two years ago, often called me a good, good girl in the earliest days of my youth. I still hear her voice saying those words and will never forget the timbre of her voice or the inflection of her words. In the years that followed in which that *good girl* was abused and then nearly decimated, I now see how that good, good girl is still resident within me today. Celebrating the survival of that good, good girl helped me to return to the activities which gave me the most joy throughout my early life—laughing, dancing, good food, and the closeness of people who know me well and love me fiercely. I now incorporate these experiences regularly into my daily life as an essential part of my recovery.

That attentive, good, good girl grew up to become a therapist who now has *all* the tools to help the girl who was once so embroiled in turmoil that she nearly perished during my attempt to self-harm. I have become the person who can now protect that little girl forevermore. **That little girl today is as attentive and watchful as ever—guiding my intuition and making sure that I fully enjoy and celebrate all the good things that come my way.**

When I dare to be powerful, to use my strength in the service of my vision, then it becomes less And less important whether I am afraid.

~AUDRE LORDE

GRATITUDE

Thank you to Aunt Rena for being the first person to tell me I should write a book.

Sonja, people say long-distance relationships don't work—but they haven't met us. Thank you for being my cousin, friend, secret-holder, and long-distance shoulder to cry on. I love you.

Thank you to my daughter, Kya. You are so smart, and so aware of people and their feelings. You also give the tightest and best hugs I've ever received. You give me the love that the little girl I was, needed but struggled to have, while growing up. I am so proud of you. I am grateful God chose me to be in your life as your momma. Each time you held me as I cried, while retelling my history of abuse, you healed so much of what I didn't know could be healed through your simple words to me of, "It's OK." When you ask if I'm *OKAY*, you will never know what that means to me. I love you, I love you, I love you.

To my husband—until I met you, I could never have fathomed that unconditional love was meant for me. I didn't know I would meet a man who wouldn't abuse or abandon me in any way. You keep proving me wrong. I will never get used to the love you give to me, our daughter, and the home we've built together. You give generously, not only to me and your family, but I also marvel at the contributions you make to the world at large. You've encouraged me every step of the way. When I worked on this book at 4:00 a.m., you understood. How, why, and when did God decide you should love me? It doesn't matter, does it? I will cherish you until the end of time. Thank you for being consistent in your love, and thank you for supporting my dreams. Thank you for being my armor, my comedian, and my true best friend. Thank you for calling me *the smartest woman you know.* Thank you for believe in me and standing by me. You are my best friend and the best decision I've ever made.

Thank you to each person who gently brought me to the point of finishing my first book by asking, "When's the book coming?" or "You still workin' on that book?" Thank you to all the Mommas I met while I was training in the military, working for the military, or attending church. You helped me understand that I am stronger and more capable than I realize.

Thank you to all the people I learned from via TV, radio, podcasts, and books. You helped to raise me, mentor, and motivate me to tell my story. This list includes Dr. Frederick K.C. Price, whose preaching I watched when I was a child in my grandmother's living room; Jesse Duplantis, who I watched when I was in high school and who helped me to laugh while learning about God's grace; and Bishop T.D. Jakes, Steven Furtick, and Joel Osteen, who all helped to grow my faith, heal my depression, teach me to accept my imperfections, and, most of all—teach me to hope. This list also includes: Glennon Doyle, Sarah Bessey, Elizabeth Gilbert, Issa Rae, Luvvie Ajayi, and Ava DuVernay, all of whom gave me the courage and inspiration to write my memoir. Christine Caine, Joyce Meyer, and Iyanla Vanzant ministered and taught me to forgive my abusers. Thank you, Oprah—you've paved the way for me. Amanda Seales, Roxane Gay, Lidia Yuknavitch—this book wouldn't be written without your voices. I needed examples of what it meant to speak in truth—to feel and express my range of emotions verbally and through my writing, and you helped me. To all of you, through your lives, you gave me a road map for healing. You reminded me that God sees, knows, and understands my pain. Thank you to all the people who lived their lives in public, wrote books, and shared their stories.

To my editors Signe, Nikki, Alison—thank you for challenging me as a first-time writer, pushing for more than I thought I had inside of me.

To Sonny you took my manuscript, rearranged it, and inserted elegance and beauty. You collaborated with me in ways I didn't know I needed. Thank you for the weeks of hard work you put into helping me find my voice. Thank you for taking detailed notes, listening to my needs and meeting every request. Most importantly, you didn't leave me alone to figure things out on my own. Your professionalism, calmness, and honesty made me feel safe with you. The communication you provided weekly let me know that you cared about my story and would be with me long after it's published. You are AMAZING, and I look forward to future collaborations.

To Mellisa, such a pleasant and welcome delight. Thank you for editing and formatting my manuscript. Thank you for your kind words, speaking from your heart, encouraging me, giving voice to my lived experience. I felt safe handing my book to you. Any doubts that rose about me telling my truth, you quickly and lovingly extinguished them. You are a gift, and I'm so thankful to have worked with you. I look forward to working with you again!

Thank you, Vanessa, for not only designing the cover and internal formatting, but you didn't stop until I was completely satisfied. Thank you for your feedback and honesty throughout this process. I'm so glad you agreed to work with me.

www.ingramcontent.com/pod-product-compliance
Lightning Source LLC
Chambersburg PA
CBHW070638150426
42811CB00050B/356

AARON SHERRITT

Persona Non Grata

AIDAN PHELAN

Foreword by Georgina Stones

Australian Bushranging

Dedicated to the memory of Aaron Sherritt,
and
to my partner in crime, Georgina.